Arabelle

To Corliss

J. Olympio

Narrated by A. N. Lopez

Arabelle

A Mile in These Shoes

outskirtspress
DENVER, COLORADO

Outskirts Press, Inc.
http://www.outskirtspress.com

ISBN: 978-1-4787-6731-2

Library of Congress Control Number: 2015918014

Outskirts Press and the "OP" logo are trademarks belonging to Outskirts Press, Inc.

PRINTED IN THE UNITED STATES OF AMERICA

Introduction

The adage says that to understand a person, you must walk a mile in their shoes. It doesn't say what you will find there, but a mile in my shoes may reveal that your burdens have been a little lighter than you thought. This book is not meant to be a fancy manuscript; perfection would rob my story of its essence. It is simply an account of a life that has at times been stranger than fiction.

I have discovered that in the journey through life, there are highways, tree-lined boulevards, forks, and many detours. If you find yourself on a bumpy path, don't wait for the road to improve. Climb over and crawl through obstacles till you find your way. You may never make it to the expressways, but you will not be stuck at a dead end either.

If my story inspires one person to look at their own unique burdens through tears and resolve to rise above them, then my time has been well spent.

Table of Contents

Chapter One

What started off as a walk along a tributary of the Potomac River in Washington DC's Rock Creek Park turned into a journey down memory lane.

A pretty blue bottle caught my attention. It was fighting to get to land. After days of heavy downpour, the river was swollen and moved rapidly, twisting and turning as it crashed against the rocks in its path. The current toyed with the bottle and let it get only so far before tossing it further downstream. That happened over and over again until the bottle finally disappeared.

Watching the bottle made me reflect on my life and the unexpected turns it has taken. I too have been tossed helplessly in life's swift currents. I have been slammed repeatedly against the banks and propelled down a predetermined course.

Years of suppressed feelings surged as I choked back tears. I thought about how far I had drifted from the aspirations of my youth. I was thousands of miles from the land of my birth and certainly far from the path I had plotted for myself.

I now live in a country that I once considered a foreign land. It is my new home and one that I still struggle to fit in. I have at times felt like an orphan, all alone in this world, when in reality I am a part of a large family.

I was born in the town of Pereira in Colombia, and I am the eighth of ten children. With seven brothers and two sisters, I was a child surrounded by family and friends. There was always plenty of laughter and raucous fun in our home, and the house was quiet only at night and at mealtimes. I cherish memories of my days at home, and I miss the chaos.

I smiled through tears as I pictured the family having dinner together. Back then when we ate, all ten children congregated around two tables, and the food quickly vanished off our plates. With that many mouths to feed, eating slowly allowed others to help themselves to your food.

My mother was the quintessential housewife; she always found work to do around the house. She spent several hours each day cooking, cleaning, and sewing. She also helped us with our homework. Looking back, I don't know how she managed to do all that work and raise ten children. She was usually so tired at the end of the day she couldn't get our names right. With ten children, there were many names to remember: Eduardo, Rodrigo, Rosalinda, Alberto, Rafael, Alejandro, Marcela, Diego, Juan Carlos, and me: Arabella.

My father was a civil engineer who frequently travelled to other regions of the country to build highways. He was a soft-spoken man, gentle and patient toward his three daughters. With his sons, however, he was a typical Colombian father:

kind yet strict. He did not "spare the rod." He would first have a conversation with the guilty party and then swiftly administer punishment with his birch whip. He kept the whip in a corner of the living room, and everyone treated it with reverence. He never hit the girls. When we did something wrong, he took us aside, put an arm around us, and talked to us sternly.

My father made sure that the boys earned good grades and did their chores around the house. They woke up at 5 a.m. each day and ground corn to make the morning meal. They split firewood, lit the outdoor wood stove, and heated water in cast-iron cauldrons for everyone to bathe. They also swept the yard, watered the plants, and fed our pets. We always had a henhouse full of chickens, and the boys cleaned the coop every morning and gathered freshly laid eggs for breakfast. After school, they tended the garden, shucked corn, did their homework, and ironed piles of laundry. My father believed that a man's place was to protect and provide for his family to the best of his ability. That, he said, came from education and from hard work, both at home and on the job.

Between my parents, we had an interesting dynamic in our home. My mother was strict with her daughters yet spoiled her sons. She was quick to take a slipper off and discipline the girls, but never laid a finger on the boys. The most she did was to make them stand in a corner for a few minutes. She had a long list of things that girls could or couldn't do, and she assigned us several tasks daily. We helped her cook, baked bread, and washed dishes. We swept and mopped floors, cleaned the bathroom, and hand-washed clothes and linens. Twice a month, we pickled vegetables, churned milk to make butter, and made several jars of jam for the family. My mother said she wanted us to be good wives and homemakers someday.

She didn't believe that the boys needed to do as much work around the house. As far as she was concerned, if her sons graduated from college and married good women, they wouldn't have to do any housework. When my father was on the road, we did most of the boys' chores in addition to ours. My sisters and I joked that our mother would have been happy with ten sons and no daughters.

We bided our time till our father returned home, and then it was our turn to kick back and let the boys work. A few times a year, my father gave us projects where we had to work together as a team. We painted the house and did carpentry: we built beds, bookcases, work tables, and sheds.

On the first Saturday of each month, we cleaned the house thoroughly. We washed windows and curtains. We stripped every bed and turned over mattresses. We beat rugs, waxed wood floors, scrubbed kitchen tiles, and polished pots and pans. After that, we worked on the yard. We used old-fashioned hoes and trowels to turn the soil, and we planted seeds. We pulled weeds, raked leaves, and trimmed hedges and shrubs. When our chores were done, we sat down to a large meal of porridge, *arepa*, empanadas, and fruit.

Chapter Two

*I*t is amazing how much the human brain holds on to. I delved deep into forgotten memories, going all the way back to when I was four years old. That was when my family moved from Pereira to Santa Rosa, a beautiful town nestled in the rolling hills of the Cordiera Centrales Mountains of Colombia.

Santa Rosa was magical. The slopes of the mountain were covered with striking shades of velvety green grass and brilliantly colored flowers. The air was clean and particularly fragrant in the mornings when the dew and sunlight bathed the vegetation.

To add to the charm, a glacier-covered volcano, Nevado del Ruiz, stood majestically in the distance. It was a few hours by mule or by horseback, but on a clear day we could see the snow-capped top glistening beneath the clouds.

Waterfalls cascaded from the surrounding mountain tops, forming huge hot springs in the foothills. Hundreds still travel to that little town each year, to experience the healing powers of the hot springs, known as Termales Santa Rosa de Cabal.

The people in Santa Rosa were not rich, and they did not live in mansions. They led simple yet enviable lives. My family lived in a bungalow surrounded by fruit trees heavy laden with papaya, mangoes, passion fruit, and bananas. A vegetable garden in the backyard held beds of tomatoes, greens, and sweet potatoes.

Volcanic soils gave rise to an abundance of plants in the area. We often went to open-air markets in equally enchanting towns nearby to purchase delectable fruits and vegetables. During those trips, my parents taught us how to select quality produce, good cuts of meat, and fresh fish. Once our grocery shopping was done, they treated us to grilled meats and ice cream. Life was a lot simpler back then.

I began my early education in Santa Rosa. Kindergarten was in a neighbor's home with twelve to fifteen other children. I remember writing numbers and the letters of the alphabet on large sheets of paper that the teacher handed out every morning. We did not do much else, but I loved school, and I felt very important when I sat at the dining table after supper to do my homework. I felt like I was already in college.

After kindergarten I attended Colegio Labure, a Catholic boarding school. I was a day student, and despite my many pleas, my parents would not let me be a boarder.

First grade was starkly different from kindergarten. We studied Spanish, arithmetic, and art. Every morning, we arrived at school to the smell of freshly baked bread and pastries.

Some of us day students would sneak into the dining hall and eat the pastries meant for boarders only. We thought that was mischievous, and it gave us a gratifying sense of adventure.

I liked my school, and I had many friends, so I was heartbroken when we had to leave that captivating town at the end of second grade. There were many tearful farewells.

While I cherish recollections of life in Santa Rosa, those memories are marred by a catastrophe that I now associate with the area. Years after we left, the Nevado del Ruiz erupted and melted the snow. The ensuing mudslide, or *lahar*, moved rapidly and covered the neighboring town of Armero. An estimated 23,000 of its 29,000 inhabitants reportedly lost their lives that day.

Emergency crews tried to free a thirteen-year-old girl who was buried up to her neck in mud. They did not have adequate tools, and the rescue operation went on for what seemed like eternity. The nation came to a standstill. People were glued to their television screens as they prayed and willed workers to pull the child out.

The workers placed a tire around her to prevent her from drowning, and then they surrounded her with wooden beams. They managed to free her from the waist up and gave her one of the beams to hold on to. They then tried to lift her out of the mud, but her legs were pinned down by debris. They eventually suspended their efforts because they risked breaking her legs.

Doctors determined that, to free the girl, they would have to amputate her legs, but given the unsanitary environment, they could not perform the surgery.

The world looked on as the child stood in the mud. Hour after hour went by. During that time, she was fed sweets and soft drinks. A reporter interviewed her, and she was able to hold a conversation. I can still hear her telling the man how much she loved her mother and her brother.

For two days, people went to bed, hoping that the ordeal would be over by the time they woke up in the morning. It dragged on, and it was very disturbing to watch. The girl grew weak and had very dark circles around her eyes. She eventually stopped talking, but those eyes pleaded silently with the adults to help her. People stopped their young children from watching television because it was traumatizing for them.

After sixty hours, the girl drew her last breath with television cameras looking on. Collective groans and gasps echoed around every town, and people cried openly in the streets. It was later reported that, based on the advice of doctors, the authorities had decided much earlier on to let her die. That was allegedly the most humane thing to do.

When the girl's body was finally freed, it was discovered that her aunt's legs were wrapped around hers. That and the weight of their fallen roof had prevented workers from pulling her out sooner and possibly saving her life.

It is hard to believe that a tragedy of that magnitude could come out of such an enchanting area. In my dark hours, I think of that young girl. Help was close, yet not close enough.

Chapter Three

After living in a place like Santa Rosa, it was difficult to settle down in Pereira. I missed my friends and the beautiful town we left behind. My parents enrolled me in the Escuela Boyaca, a public school run by the Catholic Church. I hated being the new kid in class, but I soon made friends.

My teacher was Doña Ester, and she taught me from the third grade to the fifth grade. In the Colombian public school system, kids have only one teacher throughout their years in elementary school. The same teacher follows a group of kids from the first grade to the fifth grade and teaches all subjects.

Science, literature, history, music, algebra, and geometry were added to the curriculum. I spent my evenings memorizing multiplication tables and studying for weekly tests. We were also taught to sew and knit, and we had to master those skills at every stage before progressing to the next grade.

My high school education was at the Colegio La Ensenanza, a private Catholic school. High school in Colombia goes from the sixth grade to the twelfth. You go from being a kid to being thrust into a school with young adults. You learn to survive.

The work load in high school was grueling and required constant studying. We had no open-book tests, we did not use calculators during exams, and there were very few multiple-choice questions. Science was my favorite subject, and all my teachers were certain that I would someday study medicine.

I also liked geography and enjoyed learning about other continents. I dreamed about visiting far-off lands when I became a physician.

I fondly remember my classmates Alicia, Marta, Liliana, and Carmenza. We loved school and challenged each other to do better. Just thinking about them makes me nostalgic for the peace of those days. We usually gathered in Alicia's house to do our homework, study for tests, and chat for hours. We would then walk one person home, only for them to walk back with the rest of the group. We would walk someone else home, and they would do the same thing. We would repeat the process until it got dark, and then we would run to our respective homes.

I wish I could go back in time to my childhood and my father's quiet voice of reassurance. He was always able to calm my fears and put a smile on my face.

I was in high school when my father was forced to retire from the civil service. He and a colleague were let go because the government supposedly wanted younger engineers with new ideas. Naturally, my father felt slighted. He had served the government for almost thirty five years and had willingly worked in remote regions that others had avoided. For two years, we struggled financially, and there were days when we had hardly any food in the house.

Fortunately for my parents, only my younger brothers and I lived at home. My older siblings had all left home by then. Eduardo and Alberto were studying in the Canary Islands. Rafael and Alejandro were completing mandatory military service. Rodrigo was enrolled in an electrical engineering program in a college near Pereira. Rosalinda was married with two children and lived in a town nearby. Marcela lived with Rosalinda and took care of her kids while she was at work in a department store.

My father eventually returned to work when my godfather gave him a job at the Registrar General's Department. He worked there for a little over a year, and things greatly improved.

When the government found out that my father was working, he was given the choice to go back into retirement or continue working and lose his pension. Their premise was that my father was drawing two government checks consecutively. It was not an uncommon practice, so my father was upset that he had been singled out. He concluded that he had somehow become a target, so he opted to keep his pension and resigned from the position.

My godfather hired Rosalinda to replace my father. Anything can happen in the Colombian government! A 24-year-old with no experience was hired to take over a mid-level managerial position from her father. Never mind that her father should not have been hired in the first place.

Rosalinda stepped into the position, with my father coaching her from behind the scenes. She supported the family with a portion of her salary, and my dad took consulting jobs to supplement his retirement income.

With more time and money at his disposal, my father was relaxed and turned his attention to his youngest children. He taught us mathematics, checked our homework, and helped us prepare for tests.

We spent hours discussing my ambition to attend medical school, and that topic always brought a smile to his face. We looked at world maps and talked about countries we wanted to visit together.

We planned to see the Alps in Switzerland, the *fjords* in Norway, the pyramids in Egypt, the rugged coastlines of New Zealand, Japan, Spain, the Rocky Mountains, the Great Wall of China, and everything in between. I was determined to become a physician so I could take my father all over the world.

Chapter Four

I was in the eighth grade when my father became ill. He had pneumonia, and after weeks of treatment his doctor recommended that he visit a place with a warm, dry climate. The weather in Pereira was always hot and humid or rainy, and that aggravated his condition.

My father went to stay with Eduardo, who was back from Spain and living in Cartagena. The weather in Cartagena was hot and dry and exactly what my father needed. He planned to be there for three months and promised to send for me when school was out.

Ten days after he left, we received a call at nine o'clock in the evening. Rodrigo was home and answered the phone. "Oh no! Oh no!" I heard him shout. Seconds later, I heard my mother wailing. I jumped out of bed and raced to the living room.

My father had just suffered a massive heart attack and died. I screamed in disbelief. "How could he possibly be dead?" I asked. How could he leave without saying goodbye? I was supposed to spend a month of my vacation with him!

What hurt most was that I had nothing to hold on to. I remember thinking that if he'd left me a message, a note, or whispered my name as he drew his last breath, it would have helped. As self-centered as it may sound, I felt cheated. My father was my favorite person, and I wanted to know that he had me in mind and would have said goodbye if he'd had the opportunity. I cried myself to sleep that night.

I had to take an exam the very next morning, and I cried the whole time. The teacher thought I was crying because I was not prepared, so she kept scolding me. One of my friends finally lost her temper and yelled at the teacher to leave me alone. Another classmate told the teacher what had happened, and she was embarrassed.

After the exam, my classmates tried to console me, and that just made me cry even more. They didn't know what it felt like to lose a father, and there was nothing they could say to ease my pain.

I went back home, where the mood was very somber. Everyone was either quiet or in tears. The television and radio were turned off, and no one was talking.

Rafael and Alejandro's military units were notified, and they were sent home that afternoon. Like the rest of us, they were in shock. Only someone who has experienced the unexpected death of a loved one knows the indescribable pain that sears through you. I cried so much I became numb.

My mother left two days later for Cartagena. None of us could go with her because she could not afford to take us.

She knew that from there on she would have to stretch every penny.

Eduardo and my mother buried my father in Cartagena. Who would have thought that when we said goodbye a few days earlier, it would be for the last time? Not attending the funeral made the loss especially difficult; I couldn't find closure.

Life as we knew it changed forever, and for years a dark cloud hung over our home. There were many nights when my mother's sobbing could be heard throughout the house.

I envied my siblings who lived outside the home, because they were able to go back to their lives. My younger brothers and I weren't quite as lucky; we had to deal with our mother's grief daily. She stayed in her room with the curtains drawn and only emerged when neighbors stopped by. She wouldn't eat and consequently lost a lot of weight. She would try to sing hymns, but that upset her even more, and she would break down and start wailing. I think she lost sight of the fact that we were also grieving.

I took charge of the home and did the cooking and cleaning. I also made sure that the boys went to school on time and did their homework. My mother received my father's pension, and that enabled me to pay the bills.

My father was only sixty years old, and just like that he was gone. Longevity was not one of the gifts given to that side of the family. His three brothers died when they were between the ages of thirty-nine and forty-two.

Arabelle:

For a long time, I believed that I would not live long. I was certain that I too would not make it past the age of forty-two. When my friends talked about the future, I said nothing because I didn't think I would be around. It took many years and a conscious effort to get over that fear.

Chapter Five

Somehow I made it through the rest of high school. I thank God that the nuns let us complete our education, even though we did not have money to pay the fees. I did well in my final exams, and I was even more determined to attend medical school. To honor my father's memory, I had to pursue my dream.

Entering medical school in Colombia was no easy feat. I first had to pass the entrance exam, and I had to score exceptionally high marks. Admission was based solely on scores, and only a small percentage of applicants were accepted into the country's few medical schools.

Higher education in Colombia is a series of eliminations, with more students cut back at each level. Very capable students are eliminated based on their performance in one exam. Eliminated students, when fortunate enough to get into schools outside the country, usually excel.

In the United States, anyone who truly wants to pursue higher education will eventually find a college that will take them.

Some countries have only a handful of accredited universities to serve their entire populations, so the competition is fierce.

I decided to work for a year so I could save money for a good preparatory program. I passed the exam, but my score was not high enough to get me into medical school. I was offered admission to the School of Engineering at the Universidad Technologica de Pereira.

A couple of friends with even lower scores were accepted into medical schools outside the country. Their parents could finance their education. I didn't have that option, so I reluctantly entered the engineering program. That is a phenomenon that students in many countries face. When they fall short of the mark and cannot study what they are passionate about, they accept what they are given.

Although I did well, I hated every minute of the engineering program. At the end of the second year, I took a bold step. I left the program and applied for jobs. My plan was to make a second attempt to get into medical school.

I took a job with the national airline, Avianca. I worked as a customer service agent at the local airport in Pereira. The job was demanding, and passengers were often rude. I was able to put up with it because I knew my situation was temporary. I was happiest when I was studying. I dreamed about hearing my name over a hospital's loudspeaker system and pictured myself as a general practitioner.

After months of studying, I took the exam, and once again my scores came in just under the mark. Again, I saw people with lower scores get into medical schools outside Colombia. I was deflated, and I felt I had let my father down.

I hear every day that you need an education to break the cycle of poverty. More often than not, you must first find money to pay for the education, and that is where the problem lies.

I didn't know what to do with my life. I continued working with the airline, though I knew I could not stay there indefinitely. I wasn't interested in any other career, and I could no longer pay for the expensive preparatory course. I was depressed for months.

After a hectic day at work, I lay in my room staring at the ceiling. My mother was crying again, and I was feeling totally discouraged. I was fed up with the gloominess in our home. That was when Rodrigo called with incredible news about scholarships available to Colombian students interested in studying in Ecuador.

At the time, enrollment in Ecuadoran universities was low, so their government was working in collaboration with the Catholic Church to recruit students from other Latin American countries.

I contacted the organization the very next day. My scores were high enough to get me into a medical school in Ecuador, so we started the application process. Before long, I gained admission into the medical school at the Universidad de Cuenca, Ecuador. My application for a scholarship was also approved.

For the first time since my father's death, I was happy. My admission to medical school brought a smile to my mother's face. She was, however, a little sad that yet another one of her children was about to leave home. Her older children had left home one after the other, in search of higher education and financial security, and not one of them had returned to settle down.

I continued to work and spent my evenings and weekends with my friends. It was good to get out of the house, and I began to feel more like a twenty-four year old and less like my mother's guardian.

Carmenza was the first in the group to learn how to drive, and she purchased an old Renault. As many as ten girls would pile into the small two-door car and drive to a friend's farm. The family let us use the top floor of the farmhouse as our hideout. It had several bedrooms and a large living room where we watched movies and listened to music.

During one of our trips, a farmhand made local rum, and we sampled it. It was my first alcoholic drink, and I remember feeling as though I didn't have a care in the world. I got up to dance, and I do not recall much else. I woke up the next day to find half of my body under the sofa and Marta's toe lodged in my ear.

We went back every Saturday and indulged in the liquor. We were a sight to behold: ten intoxicated girls laughing and danc-ing till we fell asleep on the floor, on couches, and on tables. We rarely ever made it to the bedrooms and the comfortable beds.

The farmer's wife woke us up on Sunday afternoons and gave us coffee brewed with spices to help us with our hangovers. She would then serve us a big breakfast of potatoes, eggs, ham, and sausages, topped with a very spicy salsa. After the meal, we would head for Pereira and sing all the way there.

It was soon time to leave my friends and family and head for Ecuador. I was leaving home for the very first time, and suddenly the prospect was scary. Thoughts of abandoning the program briefly crossed my mind, but becoming a physician held a greater appeal, so I pushed aside the anxiety. I knew that the sacrifice would be worth it.

On the morning I left, my friends showed up to say good-bye. After many hugs and promises to stay in touch, my mother and I left for the central bus station. She was very quiet, and I knew she was holding back tears. Thankfully, the bus was ready to leave the station when we arrived. With a hug and kiss, I climbed on board. The quick escape spared me the tearful parting that I was dreading.

I waved as we pulled out of the station and began the three-hour trip to Cali. From there, I was going to catch another bus for the six-hour trip to Pasto, spend the night with Eduardo's in-laws, and go to Cuenca on the following day.

I was excited and finally on my way. When you have to fight hard for an opportunity, you develop a hunger for success. I was eager to start school, and I was determined to be at the top of my class. I felt a little guilty about leaving my mother and my younger brothers, but I was happy to get away from the sadness that had encircled our home.

Chapter Six

The trip to Cali was an uneventful one. The ride took us through flat lands of sugar cane and pineapple plantations. We also drove past many sheep farms and cattle ranches. A mountain range loomed in the distance, and the farther we drove, the closer we got to the rugged terrain.

There were no buses going to Pasto from Cali that day; the only vehicle going there was a large cab. After a three-hour ride, I was reluctant to travel another six hours by cab. I explored my options, and since I didn't know anyone in Cali and couldn't afford a hotel, I climbed into the cab.

I was the first passenger there, and I chose the front seat. Four other passengers got in, and it took some rearranging to fit us all in the cab. There were two young sisters, a young man, and a woman. One of the sisters sat in the front, between the driver and me. Her sister sat behind the driver, and the male passenger sat in the middle, between the young girl and the woman. Once we were all seated, we set off and very soon left Cali behind.

We drove through several towns and villages, and I saw parts of the country I had never seen before. There were very remote regions where I did not see any schools, hospitals, or shops. Some villages consisted of a handful of huts, small farms, and a few grazing animals. I wondered what it would have been like to grow up in such areas. What kind of education would I have had? Would my aspirations have been different? Would I be aware of the big cities in the country? Would I know about the rest of the world? It was hard to believe that some people never left those villages and knew nothing besides their own simple existence.

We drove through steep mountainous areas with narrow, winding roads that had no barriers to keep vehicles from going over the edge. In some places, we had to stop for oncoming vehicles to get through. It was nerve-wracking to look down into the valleys far below.

In spite of the conditions, the cab driver continued to speed and at one point narrowly missed a goat. We asked him to slow down, and he just joked about the missed opportunity to take the animal home.

I closed my eyes and shut my mind to what was going on around me. I fell asleep and only woke up when we stopped for lunch. It was good to get out of the cramped cab and stretch my legs. The rest stop served a traditional meal of chicken and corn soup with rice and cabbage. I had a chance to chat with the other passengers while we ate.

The passenger who shared the front seat with me was seventeen years old, and her name was Elena. She and her younger sister Rosa were going home to Pasto. The man and lady in the back were headed to Pasto to visit their respective families. Pasto was everyone else's final destination; I was headed for a new life beyond that town.

The cab driver was anxious to get back on the road, so we ate hurriedly and continued the journey. I went back to sleep almost immediately. When I woke up, the driver informed me that we were close to Pasto. He estimated that we would arrive within an hour.

I was dozing off again when the cab swerved violently. There was a blood-curdling scream from the back seat, followed by a string of expletives from the driver.

The road had suddenly dropped down a steep hill, and the cab was fishtailing. The driver tried desperately to control the vehicle but couldn't. To make matters worse, the road dramatically narrowed to a single lane. On our left was the jagged mountainside covered with trees and boulders. Moving to the right meant toppling over the edge and certain death. Staying on the road meant colliding with an approaching bus that was only yards away. The bus driver had the same options.

The bus careened from side to side, slamming against the mountain and then veering dangerously to the edge of the road. I screamed as our cab went up the side of the mountain. We moved sideways on two wheels, grazed trees, slammed into rocks, and landed back on the road. The cab bounced from side to side, and with a deafening sound we crashed into the bus.

We were covered in broken glass, and there was a strong smell of fuel and burning tires. I was afraid the cab would burst into flames, so I desperately tried to open my door. "Help me, Lord!" I cried frantically.

Elena, who was sitting next to me, was motionless and bleeding profusely from a head wound. The rearview mirror was plastered across her forehead. Our driver was lying back against his headrest, also unmoving. I leaned in to talk to him and promptly recoiled. He had a huge gash across the forehead, and his left eyeball was hanging out of the socket. I was sick to my stomach.

The male passenger managed to climb over the woman seated behind me and opened her door. She was in shock and would not get out of the cab. The man dragged her out, and she appeared to have only minor injuries.

The man yanked my door open and pulled me out. He then helped the younger of the two sisters out of the back seat. Although Rosa was limping, she looked like she'd escaped severe injuries. When the man carried her unconscious sister out of the wreckage, Rosa became hysterical.

I looked around. The scene was horrendous. Both vehicles were so mangled, you couldn't tell the make or model of either one. Passengers were slowly climbing out of the rear of the bus.

The bus driver got out, took a look at the vehicles, and took off running. Left to fend for themselves, the passengers helped each other and carried the severely injured off the bus. Many were bleeding, and a few passengers looked lifeless.

The situation was dire, and a few of us tried to walk down the mountain to look for help. Someone commented on my injury, and that was when I realized that I had blood gushing from my forehead. I don't know how I could have missed it; my clothes were soaked with blood.

A couple of vehicles showed up and transported us to a hospital in a small town called El Bordo Cauca. The hospital was ill-equipped to take care of that many patients. It was complete chaos as they tried to triage the wounded. The cab driver and Elena were among the first to be treated.

While I was in the waiting room, I discovered that I was missing a few front teeth. I was concerned about arriving on campus with a huge gap in my mouth, but I was not going to let that deter me from going to school.

A doctor took a look at my forehead and walked away. He came back a few minutes later and stuck sutures in my pocket. Apparently, the hospital had limited supplies, and he wanted to make sure that when my turn came to be treated, they could take care of my wounds.

After an hour or so, a nurse stitched my forehead and sent me back to the waiting room. It was getting late, and I was anxious to get to Pasto. When I tried to stand up, I couldn't. My legs were swollen, and the pain was excruciating.

I spent the night in that hospital, and in the morning I was moved together with others to a hospital in Pasto. X-rays revealed that both my legs were broken. I was in utter dismay. My legs were placed in casts, from my feet to my knees. It was clear that I would not be travelling to Ecuador any time soon.

I was upset about not being able to continue my trip, so a nurse put things in perspective for me. She told me that the cab driver broke his neck and was paralyzed from the chest down. Rosa, who had been sitting behind him, didn't make it through the night. She broke her leg in three places and had died from complications. Her sister Elena died from her head injury, and a few passengers on the bus didn't make it.

Instead of exploring campus, I was lying in bed with both legs hoisted, yet I still had a lot to be thankful for. Others in the same cab ended up far worse off by virtue of where they were seated.

The hospital staff notified my family and the university in Ecuador. Rodrigo arrived three days later, and I was discharged into his care. The doctors said I would need follow-up care and I would be unable to start school for many months. Since we couldn't afford the special transport required to make the nine-hour trip to Pereira, I had to stay in Pasto.

Rodrigo made arrangements for me to stay with Eduardo's in-laws until I was well enough to go home by bus.

Before I left the hospital, rubber soles were placed at the bottom of my casts, and I managed to hobble around. I looked like a character out of a zombie movie.

Eduardo's in-laws were very kind to me. They took me to the hospital every day for physical therapy, and they found a local dentist to replace my missing teeth. That was a relief; I would gladly have gone to school with a toothless mouth had the doctors let me, yet I wasn't prepared to let my friends see me with a few missing teeth.

When some of the doctors heard that I was headed for medical school, they gave me books on Anatomy, Cell Biology, Genetics, and Biochemistry. I devoured those books.

The university allowed me to defer my start date, and that gave me something to smile about. I did everything the therapists asked me to do, so I would heal quickly.

Chapter Seven

The casts were removed after three months, and I returned to Pereira. Except for Rodrigo, no one had been able to visit me in Pasto, so it was good to see the family again.

I needed plenty of rest and months of therapy. It took me a year to fully recover from my injuries, and by then I was ready to salvage my dream. I called the university to get a start date. The person on the other end of the line calmly told me that Ecuador had discontinued the program.

It felt like ice-cold water raced through my veins. I called my contact at the Catholic Church and got the same news. I almost fainted. My brothers had to restrain me, to keep me from banging my head against the wall.

Enrollment levels in Ecuadoran universities had risen sharply, and there was no longer a need to attract foreign students. Secondly, the decades-old love-hate relationship between Colombia and Ecuador had deteriorated. Colombian guerillas had been crossing over into Ecuador and wreaking havoc on communities. Consequently, their government closed its borders to Colombians.

To say that I was disappointed or devastated would not even begin to describe how I felt. I woke up every morning, hoping the nightmare was over. The feeling of loss was comparable to what I felt when my father passed away.

My faith was challenged. After all I had gone through, I did not understand why God would take away my opportunity to pursue an education. All I had to show for my efforts, were two unbecoming scars on my forehead, an aching body, and flashbacks of a horrible accident. Medical school had eluded me once again.

It still hurts to look back on that difficult time in my life. I've often wondered why things seamlessly fall in place for some people while good fortune flees from others.

My family and friends tried to help me get through that dark period, but I just wanted to be left alone. I was not interested in contrived conversations, and I could not indulge in revelry to drown my sorrows. Things had changed, and there was no hope left. Through no fault of mine, I had lost the greatest opportunity of my life. I did not have the money, the scholarship, or the courage to try again.

I went back to Avianca Airlines and fell into a routine. I went to work, helped around the house, and slept. I didn't want to do anything else. I didn't want to be happy. I had been sentenced to a life of mediocrity, and I resigned myself to my fate.

Working at the airline was a lot more difficult because it was no longer a temporary job. I wasn't there just to save money for school; it had become a "real job" and one that I hated. It took a lot of self-restraint to be professional and not lose my temper with passengers.

Once in a while, the airline sent me out of town for training, and that broke the monotony. Six months after my return, I was selected to go to Miami. The airline got me a visa, and I took my first trip to the United States.

The city was beautiful, and the hotel was luxurious. Much as I enjoyed my surroundings, I was reminded of the dream I had been forced to give up. I'd wanted to be a physician so I could afford to visit cities like Miami.

Shortly after that trip, I left Avianca Airlines and took a new job at IBM in Pereira. The job didn't pay much. My intention was to gain computer skills, find a clerical position in a small company, and withdraw into my own little world.

Not too long after I started work at IBM, three of my older brothers came home to visit. Eduardo flew in from Cartagena. He'd married a physician, and together they had two kids. Alberto came all the way from Finland. While studying in Spain, he'd met and married a Finnish lady, and they had settled in Helsinki. Alejandro came from Montreal, where he lived with his wife and two daughters.

It was good to have so many of my siblings together again. In spite of the atmosphere, I had sad moments. My older brothers noticed and consoled me on the missed opportunity.

Alejandro and Alberto both thought it would be best for me to leave Colombia. They were still trying to find their feet in their new countries and promised to help me as soon as they could.

Two days before Alejandro left for Canada, he suggested that I go with him. I had nothing to lose, or so I thought at the time. I agreed to go to Montreal. Fortunately, my visa to the States was still valid, so we decided to fly into Miami and travel by road to Canada. Alejandro assured me that he would have no problem getting me across the Canadian border.

We discussed the matter with our mother. She had no objections, and in no time my bag was packed. I didn't tell my friends that I was leaving because I did not want any fanfare. If things did not go as planned, I wanted to be able to return and quietly go back to my routine.

With my mother's blessing, we left for Bogota, and from there we flew to Miami. We spent the night with a cousin, caught a Greyhound Bus the next morning, and headed north. I was excited and looked forward to seeing the different states along the east coast of the United States.

I felt very secure traveling with my brother. When my father died, it was as though I lost both my parents. My mother was consumed by grief, and I had to fend for myself and my younger brothers. With Alejandro to guide me, I felt things would be different. I was confident that Canada held a bright future for me.

When I realized that we would travel through the state of Virginia, I convinced Alejandro to let me visit a friend who lived there. Esmeralda was my former classmate Marta's sister. She was a year ahead of us, and she'd moved to the States shortly after graduating from high school. She was married and lived in Falls Church with her husband and daughter.

We called Esme from a rest stop in South Carolina, and she screamed when she heard my voice. We talked and laughed till Alejandro took the phone and wrote down her address and the directions to her home.

I could barely contain my excitement when we crossed into Virginia. That was short-lived. The state was much bigger than I could have imagined, and we had to drive a few more hours to get to Northern Virginia.

We drove through beautiful cities and past large, stately homes. We finally reached a Greyhound station in Springfield, where we got off the bus. We caught a cab to an area with contrastingly smaller houses and found Esme's home.

Someone opened the front door before we could even get out of the cab. It took me a few seconds to realize that the portly woman grinning from ear to ear was Esme. She looked much more mature than she had just four years earlier.

Esme was ecstatic to see us, and she convinced me to stay with her for a couple of days. My brother thought it was a good idea, and he made plans to stay with a friend in Washington while I spent time with Esme and her family.

Chapter Eight

$\mathcal{E}$sme begged me to stay with her in Virginia, and her husband Antonio also pleaded with me not to leave. His wife was lonely, and he was worried that if things remained the same, she would move back home to Colombia. They both assured me that they had a job for me and I could live with them indefinitely. After discussing the matter with Alejandro I decided to stay, and he continued the trip to Canada without me.

Two days later, I was working at the upscale Galleria Mall at Tyson's Corner. I worked as a janitor under the name Carlos Felipe Sanchez. I didn't understand how I could use a man's name, but I asked no questions. I focused on the job, thankful to earn "the almighty dollar."

I worked eighteen-hour shifts on Saturdays and Sundays, and Antonio was my supervisor. It was a beautiful mall, but when you clean restrooms from five o'clock in the morning till eleven o'clock at night, you cease to see the beauty around you.

I made $11 an hour and earned about $400 per weekend. I picked up the checks, and Antonio cashed them. Compared to what I made in Colombia, it was good money. One week's pay was equivalent to what I made in three weeks at IBM in Pereira.

From my wages, I paid Antonio $80 a week for giving me the job. I also gave him $120 every week for the tiny room I shared with their daughter. An additional $50 went towards food. I wanted to work full time and work slightly shorter shifts, but Antonio had other janitors working under the same name and on different days of the week. Moreover, he had other plans for me. I was their unpaid nanny and maid. From Monday to Friday, I took care of their daughter while Esme was at work. I cooked, cleaned the house, and hand-washed clothes.

I soon became disillusioned about working at the mall. People treated me like I was invisible or simply insignificant. I would greet customers who came into the restrooms, and very few of them acknowledged me. Some brushed against me, others shooed me out of the way, and on several occasions people swore at me for no apparent reason.

I never envisioned myself cleaning bathrooms at a shopping mall. I wondered what the nuns at my high school would say if they saw me. What would my friends back home think? I prayed that nobody from Pereira would see me in my new role.

Before long, I started feeling alienated. I didn't know anyone in the area besides Esme and Antonio. We didn't have cable television, so we didn't get Spanish channels, and since

I didn't speak English, I never knew what was going on around me or in the rest of the world.

To make matters worse, just weeks after my arrival, I started feeling uncomfortable in Esme's home. She became withdrawn, and Antonio barely spoke to me, unless it was to give me more tasks around the house. I had nobody to talk to, and the only time I interacted with others was at work. Even though it was limited interaction, it was better than the awkward silence in Esme's house.

All members of the Galleria cleaning crew were from Latin America, and I soon realized that though everyone supposedly spoke Spanish, there were many regional accents and dialects. It was also glaring that we came from greatly varying socioeconomic backgrounds.

Some of the workers were clearly uneducated and were from rural areas of Latin America. Their grammar was poor, they had limited vocabulary, and their Spanish was mixed with indigenous languages. I was often taken aback by their expressions and mannerisms, which were sometimes crude. For example, I was raised to use euphemisms for certain bodily functions, so I found it shocking that their norm was to use graphic language for the same. Since our jobs entailed the cleaning of bathrooms, there was plenty of opportunity for very crude words to come up in their conversations.

Other members of the team seemed to have basic education, and that was to be expected. They came from different cities and towns in search of a better life. A few of the workers seemed very well-educated, and I wondered what their stories were. My guess was that they were doing janitorial work until they could get work permits. I didn't ask any questions because I didn't want anyone to question me about my situation.

In the immigrant community, asking questions makes people uncomfortable. They do not divulge personal information because there is always the fear of blackmail when friendships turn sour. Confidants with legal status have been known to call the authorities when things go wrong.

Late one night, I overheard two co-workers talking. They spoke freely because they thought nobody could hear them. It was evident that they were being exploited and most of the money they earned went to others. They hadn't been able to save any money, so even though they wanted to go back home, they couldn't.

The immigrant's creed is that you do not go back home empty-handed. That notion is what keeps people hanging on for years. Every new immigrant plans to save money quickly and return to their country. Unfortunately, that rarely happens. They get sucked into the system; they are unable to progress and unable to return home.

Given the arrangement with Antonio, I knew I wouldn't save much money if I stayed with them. I made a mental note to move out as soon as it was feasible. If things didn't work out, I would go to Canada or back to Colombia.

Conditions in Esme's home steadily worsened. Antonio became more demanding, and he was always angry. Esme was unhappy, and when her husband was not around, she sang sad songs about being far from home. She confided in me that she was tired of the charade. She had very little in common with her husband, and she wanted to go back to Colombia.

Esme had met Antonio when he was visiting Pereira. He'd returned six months later to ask for her hand in marriage. Though her family had been against the marriage, the idea of moving to the United States was so enticing, Esme defied her parents.

When she arrived in Virginia, she realized that she'd made a mistake. Antonio's life was nothing like he'd described to her back in Pereira. By then, it was too late; she was pregnant. She felt misled and resented her husband.

Esme wanted to leave Antonio, but she didn't have the means to go back home. After keeping her misery from her family for years, she was ready to ask for their forgiveness and their help.

Back in Colombia, I heard about young women who met and married men returning home on vacation from other countries. The men were usually well-dressed and seemed prosperous. They had pictures of themselves outside beautiful buildings, in expensive vehicles, and at festive events in far-off places. That was all part of the strategy to attract women who were otherwise out of their league. Many young ladies fell for the façade and did not discover the truth until much later. By then, they were far from home and unable to return.

Those seemingly prosperous men often worked two or three jobs just to survive in their new countries of residence. They left home at the crack of dawn and did not return till late at night. Home was usually a cramped little space. The fancy clothes were purchased by making small deposits on the items, followed by several payments.

Esme's story was a classic example of that phenomenon. When she met Antonio, he gave her the impression that he ran a successful business in Virginia. Once she joined him, she found out that life for him was a struggle and entailed many scams. She lived in constant fear that the police would knock on their door someday and arrest them.

I did what I could to keep Esme's spirits up. We sometimes went for long walks. While that helped her, it did the exact opposite for her husband. The tension in the home mounted. Antonio became openly hostile and accused me of driving a wedge between him and his wife.

Though the situation grew volatile, I stayed because I did not have anywhere else to go. Esme and Antonio openly argued about everything: bills, food, laundry, work, their daughter, and, of course, me. Every issue was a good enough reason for contention. Behind closed doors they would yell at each other, and then Antonio would storm out of house, slamming doors behind him. On one occasion, he threw a mug against the wall and shattered it. That scared me, and I knew I had to leave. By then, my visa had expired, so crossing the border into Canada was out of the question. I had very little money, and I was not ready to return to Colombia.

I tried not to aggravate Antonio, and I stayed out of sight when he was home. I desperately wanted to call Alejandro and let him know what was going on, but I couldn't. Today, everyone has a cell phone, and phone cards can be purchased almost everywhere. It was different back then. There were no cell phones or phone cards, just land lines and pay phones.

Making international calls was a challenge for me. I couldn't call from Esme's phone, and when I tried to use a payphone, the instructions were in English and I had no idea what was said.

I later found out that Alejandro had called several times during that period, and each time, Antonio gave him the impression that I was at work or sightseeing with Esme.

Chapter Nine

*D*uring my lunch break one Saturday, a co-worker struck up a conversation with me. She was from Bolivia, and her name was Gladys. Back in her country, she was a pharmacist. In the United States, she cleaned floors and toilets for a living.

Gladys sensed that I was unhappy. She did not ask questions, and she mentioned no names. She spoke in generalities and stressed that to make any progress in America, I would have to become more independent. That meant learning to speak English and learning to use the public transportation system.

Over the next few weeks, Gladys took me under her wing. We went to the West Falls Church Metro station, where she taught me how to purchase train tickets. She explained the Washington DC transit system and showed me how to navigate from one train to another and from bus to bus. Seemingly easy things, until you try to do it in a large metropolis and in a language you do not understand.

Gladys also took me to a school where I enrolled in a free program to learn the English language. While I was excited at the prospect of learning to speak English, I knew that breaking the news to Esme and her husband could potentially cause problems. I figured that Esme would be happy for me; Antonio on the other hand would consider it another ploy to influence his wife. Esme spoke hardly any English, and I had a strong feeling that her husband wanted to keep it that way. Whenever she tried to read or pronounce English words, he would make disparaging comments and tell her that she would never learn the language.

Since the class did not start for a few weeks, I kept the news to myself. There was no reason to stir up trouble until it was absolutely necessary to do so.

Antonio sent me to a bank to cover for a janitor who was sick. The bank was closed and the lights were off. I waited outside for over an hour, hoping someone would show up and unlock the door. A Latina arrived and let me into the building, but I still couldn't get into the bank. We talked briefly, and I was shocked to learn that she was from my hometown of Pereira. Her name was Yolanda, and we bonded instantly. We put a note on the door of the bank stating where I could be found, and then we went to the floor she was working on. No one came by to look for me, and I ended up helping Yolanda to clean several offices that night.

Yolanda had a fascinating story. She had paid a Colombian who assured her that he knew a safe and easy way to smuggle her into the United States via Mexico. After extorting money from her and from a few others, the man took them on what turned out to be a terrifying journey. They crossed a river in the middle of the night, wading through waist-deep water, climbing over rocks, and crawling through a ravine on their stomachs.

Yolanda arrived in the country soaking wet, with fractured ribs, sprained ankles, and lacerations all over her body. Her feet and hands were bruised and swollen, and all her toenails and fingernails were broken.

Two men were waiting for the group on the other side of the river. They charged each person a fee and led them down a dark path to a pickup truck hidden in a thicket. The travelers were dropped off near a bus terminal somewhere in Texas. A lady in the group was going to her relatives in Virginia, and even though Yolanda didn't know anyone there, she took the long bus ride with the woman.

I'd heard many stories of women being robbed, raped, and even killed by those who promised to bring them into the country and deliver them safely to their loved ones. Fortunately for Yolanda, she was spared that. After surviving the trip, she was determined to carve out a good life for herself.

Though Antonio never sent me back to that location, I stayed in touch with Yolanda. I think God used the failed assignment to cross our paths because he knew I needed a friend. Yolanda knew Esme and Antonio and didn't care for the man. She said people like Antonio tried to keep new immigrants isolated because that made them easier to control.

Yolanda had been living in Virginia for seven months and knew her way around. For someone who had not been in the country for a long time, she knew the loopholes in the system. She helped me to open a bank account and promised to help me get a Social Security card. Like Gladys, she encouraged me to learn to use the transit system.

I eventually told Esme that I had enrolled in an English class and planned to get a Social Security card. She was excited and wanted to take the English class too. When she mentioned it to her husband, he was enraged.

Antonio must have ranted incessantly for at least three hours. Once again, he accused me of trying to influence his wife. He asked me to move out and told me that I was fired from my cleaning job.

Throughout the tirade, I said nothing. I did not want to further provoke him, lest he throw me out that night. I hid in my room and prayed that after letting off steam, Antonio would change his mind about firing me.

I went to work the next morning. I was so nervous I felt sick. I had never lived in a contentious environment, so I found the situation extremely stressful. I kept looking over my shoulder, afraid that Antonio would show up and escort me off the premises.

I didn't mind the long shift that day; I dreaded going back to the house. My prayer that Gladys would show up for the evening shift went unanswered. I contemplated sleeping in a supply room but decided against it. I figured that with my luck, a security guard would find me, Antonio would swear he didn't know me, and I would be arrested and deported.

I got home just before midnight, and my intention was to let myself in quietly and go straight to bed. Even though it's been several years, I still get emotional when I remember that night.

My suitcase was sitting on the curb, and my belongings were strewn all over the grass. My chest tightened and my body shook uncontrollably from fear. I had no idea where I was going to sleep that night.

Passersby had rummaged through my things and taken what they wanted. I looked frantically for my family photographs, but they were all gone. I sat on the curb and slowly folded the few clothes I had left. I placed them in the suitcase and walked away with no particular destination in mind. Only someone who has been through the pain and humiliation of eviction can understand how dejected I felt.

It was almost one o'clock in the morning; there were no hotels nearby, and I wasn't carrying much money anyway. I didn't have Gladys or Yolanda's phone numbers with me, and there was no one to call. I prayed for a miracle and prayed that the police would not drive by. The last thing an illegal immigrant wants is an encounter with the police. Antonio often said that as an illegal immigrant, even if you are struck by a vehicle, as long as you can move, you must get up and disappear before the police arrive.

I could see the lights from the small shopping area nearby, and I headed there. I thought it would be the safest place to wait for morning.

I was surprised to find the convenience store open. Apparently, it was open twenty-four hours a day. I went in with the intention of lingering for as long as I possibly could.

I could not believe my ears when someone called out my name. My prayers had been answered! It was Yolanda. She had been on her way home from a part-time job when she had gotten the urge to stop for a snack. Without a doubt, that was my God looking out for me!

I went home with Yolanda, and she was such a blessing to me. Her roommate had just moved out after paying a full month's rent. She let me have the room free of charge, and she contacted her friends to see if anyone knew of job openings.

Yolanda really did have connections in the right places, and as promised, she helped me get a Social Security card. She then pushed me to take driving lessons. I didn't think I could ever drive on the highways of Virginia, but Yolanda was persistent. She helped me study for the written test and gave me driving lessons. She then introduced me to a driving instructor who gave me additional lessons at a discount.

Six weeks after I left Esme's home, I had a Social Security card, a driver's license, and I was learning to speak English. I was driving around Washington and enjoying the nation's capital. I loved walking along the tidal basin and visiting the monuments and memorials on the National Mall. It is amazing how much more you appreciate your surroundings when you are happy.

When one of Yolanda's friends had to go to El Salvador, she asked me to cover for her. Maria worked as a nanny in Bethesda, Maryland, and her application for a green card had just been approved. Back then, when an illegal alien became eligible for a green card, they had to exit the country, pick up the card, and re-enter legally.

Maria introduced me to her employers, and they hired me temporarily. The Levensons were a young couple; they were both attorneys, and they had two children. Even with my limited English, we were able to communicate, and they made me feel at home.

Two weeks went by quickly, and before I knew it, Maria was back. She came back rejuvenated. She had been separated from her family for six years, and the trip seemed to have done wonders for her. She had many plans, and with her green card in hand, she was ready to explore the possibilities.

I was puzzled to hear that finding another job was at the top of Maria's list of things to do. I didn't understand why she would leave her sponsors right after they got her the green card. Her explanation was that she needed to spread her wings. Even though that didn't sound right to me, I kept my opinions to myself.

I returned to Yolanda's apartment, but not for long. A friend of hers told us about an Argentine family that was looking for a live-in housekeeper. They lived in Potomac, Maryland,

and since the area was not easily accessible by bus or train, Yolanda drove me to the interview. She was eager to meet the family and put in a good word for me, but she was asked to wait outside.

It was a big, beautiful home with high ceilings, expensive-looking chandeliers, and gorgeous marble floors. The room where I was interviewed had exquisite furniture and silk rugs, and expensive art hung on every wall. The family consisted of a doctor, his stay-at-home wife, and their three daughters aged nine, seven, and two. The couple had a nanny for the children. The housekeeper's job would be to cook, serve meals, wash and iron clothes, and clean the house. It sounded easy enough, and I assured them that, given the opportunity, I would do a great job.

The nanny was also Latina, and I wanted to know which country she was from. I was not introduced to her, and we did not get a chance to speak. When she was asked to let me out, she walked ahead of me and hastily ushered me through the door. Before I could say a word, she smiled pleasantly and shut the door. I found the behavior odd, but I did not dwell on it. I was excited at the prospect of a full-time job with a Spanish-speaking family. I prayed that the couple would hire me.

Chapter Ten

For the next two days, I stayed close to the phone. The call came on the third day, and Dr. Morales offered me the job. Although the pay was less than the going rate, I accepted it. He asked me to report in three days, and before I could thank him for the opportunity, he hung up.

I scrambled to do laundry and pack my bags. With Yolanda's help, I found an English program in Maryland. I planned to take a class one evening a week and on Saturday afternoons. I would have to catch two buses to get to the class, yet I was prepared to do so. I had a live-in job, an opportunity to continue learning the English language, and a place to go to on weekends. I was happy.

Yolanda dropped me off at the Morales home on my first day. She wanted to meet Mrs. Morales, but the nanny informed us that the lady was not available. When we tried to hold a conversation with the young woman, she politely told us that there was something she had to attend to. With that, Yolanda wished me luck and left.

I waited for a couple of hours before Mrs. Morales came downstairs. I got up and smiled when she walked into the kitchen. With a nod of the head, she handed me uniforms that I was to wear at all times. She went over my duties, which had greatly increased since the interview.

Before I could say anything, she thrust a kitchen towel in my hand and told me to clean the kitchen counter. She asked the nanny to show me where to find cleaning supplies and told me to mop the floor. She then stalked off, leaving me confounded.

I have always considered myself a hard worker, and given the chores we did at home, I was no stranger to housework. However, the amount of work that I had to do in the Morales household was incredible. I worked like a slave. My hours were from six in the morning till eleven at night.

So much for speaking the same language! I quickly learned that my employers were not interested in holding conversations with me.

When I interviewed for the job, I thought they were a quiet couple. In working for them, I realized that they were not quiet at all—they were just very selective about whom they talked to. I was the help, and I spoke only when I was spoken to. They snapped their fingers to get my attention and barked sharp orders in rapid succession. I scuttled around just to keep up with the tasks.

Dr. Morales had a private practice in neighboring Chevy Chase, though he spent a significant amount of time at home and on the golf course. Mrs. Morales, or Señora Morales as she preferred to be addressed, spent most of her time watching television or on the phone. The two younger children were pleasant, but the oldest was demanding and sometimes downright obnoxious. Thankfully, I did not have to interact much with the little diva.

My day began with making breakfast for the family. There was a specific menu for each day of the week. After serving breakfast, I cleaned the house. Señora Morales wanted her house to be impeccable at all times, so I vacuumed, scrubbed, and waxed floors all day. I also dusted, washed windows, swept patios, and raked leaves.

When I took a break from cleaning, it was to cook lunch and dinner. Every meal had to be cooked to perfection. The presentation had to be aesthetically pleasing, and for each meal, I set the table as though the Queen of England were coming to dine.

After serving dinner, I washed and ironed clothes till I collapsed onto my bed from exhaustion. There was always laundry to be done in that house. I changed bed sheets and towels daily, and the family changed clothes at least three times a day.

Dr. Morales liked his clothes washed and pressed a certain way. Initially, I had to iron his shirts over and over again because no matter how hard I tried, Señora Morales was never satisfied. She would ball up the clothes and throw them at me, and I would have to start all over again.

I thought I would have a nervous breakdown. The nanny finally came to my rescue and taught me how to iron Dr. Morales's clothes. When the couple was out, she would iron the doctor's shirts for me.

The nanny's name was Giovanna, though I still think of her simply as "the nanny." The girl had completely lost her identity. Somewhere in a far-off land, she had a family that loved her. In the Morales household, she was insignificant. She was just someone who moved around the house, quietly carrying out task after task. Neither the insults of a spoiled child nor the constant orders of the parents seemed to affect Giovanna. She did not yet have her papers, so no matter how badly she was treated, she was prepared to deal with it.

When you are new to a place and have few options, you hold on to a job regardless of the indignities you suffer. You work hard and bide your time. Like many immigrants, Giovanna was stuck in that phase. Years had gone by, and she was still waiting for a time when things would miraculously improve so she could dust herself off and resume living. Until then, she was content to merely exist from day to day.

Both Gladys and Yolanda had warned me about giving up on life and accepting whatever was thrown at me. I resolved to keep looking till I found a better job. I wasn't going to stay, hoping that Dr. Morales would someday sponsor me so I could get a green card. After all, Giovanna had been working for them for eight years and didn't have hers. They had to have known that she would leave as soon as she got the green card.

People are quick to complain when they are mistreated by someone of a different race. Sometimes, it is your own kind that dishes out the worst treatment. We were all from South America and spoke the same language, yet the couple treated Giovanna and me as if we were of an inferior race.

I stayed with the family for six months, and it truly was modern-day slavery. I worked seven days a week, and except for when we went grocery shopping, I did not leave the house. I wasn't able to attend a single English lesson while I worked for them. When I mustered enough courage to mention the class to Mrs. Morales, she merely looked down her nose at me and threw her head back in disdain.

Their attitude constantly reminded me of just how different my life could have been if I had made it to Ecuador and into medical school. Like Dr. Morales, I too could have been a physician, yet there I was, cleaning his home like an indentured servant.

I felt isolated from the rest of the world. There were no pay phones in the neighborhood, and we didn't dare use the Morales's phone. I was so terrified of them that I couldn't even make local calls to Gladys or Yolanda.

Looking back, I said some of my best prayers during my time in that house. I asked God to give me a job where I would feel wanted.

I wrote to my mother, Yolanda, and Gladys when I could find the time, but I did not tell them about my situation. Even though I gave my letters directly to the mailman, I was afraid that somehow Señora Morales would intercept my mail.

Giovanna and I were always on the lookout for the mailman. His arrival was the highlight of our day, and one of us would rush to meet him. We were like prisoners desperately waiting on letters from the outside.

Walking up the driveway, we would quickly yet discreetly go through the mail and take out any letters we may have received. Giovanna warned me that if Señora Morales saw our mail, she would read it and tear it up.

One day while the family was out, I ventured to call Yolanda. As luck would have it, Maria was leaving her job with the Levenson family, and they wanted me to replace her permanently.

I made a quick call to let Maria know that I was interested in the job, and we agreed on a time for me to meet with the Levensons. I had to ask my employers for time off, and I agonized over that for a couple of days. I finally told them that I had to send medication to my mother, and they gave me a few hours to do so.

Yolanda picked me up at the bottom of the road and drove me to the Levenson home. While the Levensons were happy to see me, they were concerned that I still didn't speak much English. After speaking only Spanish for six months, my English was probably worse than before.

I was so desperate to get out of the Morales home; I found enough English words to assure them that if they hired me,

I would learn the language. They took a chance on me and asked me to return in three weeks to work as their live-in nanny. The wages were generous, and I looked forward to working for them.

It took a week to find the strength to tell Dr. and Mrs. Morales that I was leaving. They were enraged. Dr. Morales said I was ungrateful, and Señora Morales shrieked and said they were well rid of me. I am sure they would have liked to fire me on the spot, but they needed someone to do the work. They decided to get all they could out of me. My workload tripled, and nothing I did was good enough.

Giovanna and I walked on eggshells till I left. I was careful to keep my distance so she would not be perceived as my co-conspirator. I did not want to make her life any more difficult than it already was. She assured me that she would be okay. She had seen several housekeepers come and go, and each time someone left, the same drama ensued.

Yolanda was there to pick me up on my last day, and she had to wait outside in the sweltering heat for two hours. Mrs. Morales was home to make sure I finished the many last-minute tasks she assigned me. Then and only then did she pay me. I thanked her for the time I spent with them and promised to call her. She knew I was being facetious, and that infuriated her. She glared at me and snorted. It was so comical I laughed out loud.

Giovanna gasped and scuttled off. She could not believe her eyes. I laughed so hard, tears streamed down my face. Señora Morales looked like she was going to combust. I slapped my sides, blew her a kiss, and literally hopped out of the room. I slammed the door behind me; I was no longer afraid of her.

I felt liberated when we pulled out of their driveway for the last time. I turned up the radio in Yolanda's car and sang at the top of my voice.

After a few minutes, Yolanda turned off the music so she could hear about my six-month ordeal. The only thing that surprised her about my experience was the fact that Mrs. Morales hadn't threatened to call the immigration authorities. That was one of the tactics employers used to keep illegal aliens in line. I was thankful that Mrs. Morales hadn't done that because I would have been forced to stay and continue working for them.

Yolanda treated me to lunch and then drove me to the Sandz School in Washington DC, where I enrolled in yet another English-language program.

Chapter Eleven

I started work at the Levensons' the following week. They told me their expectations, reminded me of the Jewish traditions they observed, and then gave me the latitude to do my work. One of my duties was to take their children to school. Even though I had a license issued by the State of Virginia, I had to take two weeks of driving lessons before they allowed me to drive their kids.

I was only required to take care of the children, yet I voluntarily did housework. It was a completely different environment, and I was happy to go the extra mile. I got the kids ready in the mornings, drove them to school, and did chores till it was time to pick them up and take them to their extracurricular activities.

In spite of their high-powered jobs, the Levensons were down to earth. Unlike my previous employers, they insisted that I call them by their first names, Josh and Laura. They didn't bark orders at me; they talked to me and treated me with respect. We ate together in the evenings, and I chatted with them before retiring to my room. Laura would kick back with a bottle of beer and tell me about her day at work. She had a great sense of humor and made me laugh constantly. I met other members of their family, and they were just as pleasant.

I was allowed to use the Levensons' phone to call Gladys and Yolanda, and they were allowed to visit me at the home. On special occasions, Laura allowed me to call my mom in Colombia.

I worked Monday through Friday, took English lessons on Saturday mornings, and spent the rest of my weekends with Yolanda and Gladys. We cooked South American dishes and went to shopping malls.

I avoided the Tyson's Corner mall because it still held painful memories for me. I also wanted to stay away from places where I could potentially run into Esme's husband Antonio. I was still afraid that he would report me to the immigration authorities and have me deported.

The girls and I went to the movie theatres a couple of times, and while I loved watching movies back in Colombia, I found the experience in English very frustrating. Before I became fluent in the language, I thought English speaking actors and actresses spoke too fast, and I could not understand them. Yolanda and Gladys weren't much better than me. At the end of a movie, we would have three different interpretations of what we saw. I resorted to buying Spanish movies and those with Spanish subtitles.

A month and a half after I started working for the Levensons, Laura found out that she was pregnant. She was worried that I would leave, but I was excited by the news.

It turned out to be a very difficult pregnancy, and in the fifth month she was put on bed rest. She worked from home, and I did my best to make her comfortable. She and I forged a strong friendship during that time.

Laura was interested in my future, and when I told her that I had almost gone to medical school, she promised to help me salvage part of my dream. America, she told me, was truly a land of opportunity, and as long as I set goals and pursued them, I could still be successful. She emphasized that it was a country where eighty-year-old grandmothers could sit in class with twenty-year-olds, if they so desired.

Laura pointed out various careers in the medical field which I could still pursue. Nursing seemed like a great option, and the more I researched it, the more excited I became. She sent me to the local community college to speak to a guidance counselor. I got pertinent information, and we decided that once her baby was a few months old, I would take prerequisite courses at night. In the interim, she pushed me to improve my English.

We counted down the months as we waited for the baby to arrive. Laura continued to drink her daily bottle of beer and disregarded my words of caution. She said her job was stressful, so she needed a drink to help her relax. Besides, she didn't think one drink a day could cause any harm.

Laura went into labor a month early and prematurely delivered a baby girl. The baby was small yet adorable. She had pretty blue eyes and absolutely no hair. I instantly fell in love with her. Laura and Josh named her Melissa.

Melissa had to remain in the hospital for a few days because she had fetal alcohol syndrome. Though we never discussed the subject, I could tell that Laura felt guilty. She tried to make up for it by giving Melissa her full attention. When she went back to work, she called constantly and she rushed home to her baby every evening. I would attend to the older children and retire to my room.

When Melissa was three months old, her pediatrician voiced concerns because she was not meeting developmental markers. She did not move her hands and legs much, she could not grasp objects, and she could not raise her head and chest when we placed her on her stomach. After several tests, she was referred to pediatric specialists at the Kennedy Krieger Institute in Baltimore. More tests were conducted, and the doctors recommended physical therapy.

Taking Melissa for therapy in addition to my other duties kept me busy, and before I knew it, the year was almost over. Melissa's health changed our focus, and I shelved my plans to start nursing school. I had no regrets; I wanted to devote my time to the little girl.

In December of that year, my brother Rodrigo, his wife, and their two children stopped to see me on their way back to Calgary from Colombia. My sister Marcela came with them, and the Levensons graciously let all five of them stay at their house. Laura insisted that they had enough room for everyone.

I drove her long distances to see doctors and therapists. I massaged her limbs twice a day and did exercises the therapists recommended. She did not sleep much, and she cried a lot, so I had to hold her constantly. To get her to sleep, I usually had to take her out in her stroller for hours at a time. The situation was taxing on the whole family, and there were many nights when we all went to bed exhausted.

I was not willing to accept the doctor's findings. I prayed constantly and asked God to heal Melissa. I talked to her day and night. I spoke to her in English and in Spanish and implored her to defy the odds.

Melissa started school before she turned two, and I took her to the program daily. I stayed with her and annoyed the teachers to no end. I made sure that they cut no corners where she was concerned.

Speech and language therapy were added to Melissa's regimen. I watched the therapists closely, and I went over the routines with her every evening and on weekends.

The therapists warned me not to speak Spanish to Melissa because they thought hearing two languages would be confusing for her. I ignored their warnings. I was passionate about taking care of her, and when I am emotional, I express myself best in Spanish.

Melissa slowly made progress. She was almost 28 months old when she started talking. She said only a few words at a time, but two months later she shocked everyone when she spoke a full sentence in Spanish. It was encouraging, and it made me even more determined to help her reach her potential. I lived for that little girl. I was there for her first swimming lesson, I taught her to ride a tricycle, and I continued to take her to play groups and to doctor's appointments. Her parents and grandparents were very appreciative of my efforts.

At some point, the school kicked me out. They'd had enough of me, and I was no longer allowed to sit in class with Melissa. I was upset, but there was nothing I could do about it.

The first couple of weeks were difficult for me because I worried about Melissa the entire time she was at school. Laura came up with a brilliant idea to hire me part-time at their law firm. I worked flexible hours and scheduled my workday around Melissa. The job gave me the opportunity to polish both my English and my clerical skills while earning more money.

The law firm was converting paper files into an electronic format, and my job was to input the data. I learned a lot about the legal system as I browsed through case files. I enjoyed the professional environment and appreciated the Levensons even more.

Josh and Laura allowed me to pursue other interests in my free time, so I took a couple of jobs cleaning homes in the neighborhood. The extra income allowed me to send a decent amount of money home to my mother every month. I regularly put money in my savings account, and I had the funds to entertain family members who visited Marcela and me.

The Levensons graciously opened their home to my family time and time again. Alberto and his family visited from Finland, Rodrigo and his family came back often, and my aunt and her family visited from New York. Conversely, when the Levensons and I were in New York, we stayed with my aunt.

During one holiday season, we had so many relatives visiting us; there were seventeen people in the Levenson home for about a week. Laura gave us free rein of the house, and the only room that was off limits was her bedroom. Even though they were Jewish, she put up a Christmas tree for us. There was plenty of food and alcohol, and we ate, drank, and sang carols together.

My mother visited us in April of 1993, and Marcela and I met her at Washington Dulles International Airport. I hadn't seen her since I left Pereira, so I expected a joyful reunion. Instead, it was a tearful one. Marcela and I flew into her arms, and we all wept freely.

Over the years, I'd spent many quiet moments wondering if I would ever see my mother again. I feared that something would happen to her, and I would be unable to return to Colombia. It was a real fear that I'd harbored for a long time, so it was surreal to see and touch her.

It is every illegal alien's worst nightmare, to get word of a loved one's illness or death back home. You either leave on a one-way ticket knowing you cannot return, or you opt not to go and live with your decision. I had often debated mentally what I would do if I had to make that hard choice.

Once we got the tears out of the way, we tried to catch up on the time we'd been apart. Our mother told us about our younger brothers at home and about friends and neighbors in Pereira.

Halfway home, she disclosed that she was nervous about staying with the Levensons. She'd never met them and thought it was an imposition. Once we got to the house, she was more at ease. The Levensons went to great lengths to welcome her. Looking back, not too many nannies were as fortunate as I was. The Argentine family would never have allowed my family members to stay in their home.

We took my mother sightseeing, and she fell in love with Washington. Though she didn't want much, we took her shopping and bought her many gifts. At the end of her trip, she was beaming.

Chapter Thirteen

The years flew by uneventfully, and I continued to work for the Levensons. In 1996, I received a letter inviting me to an interview at the Immigration and Naturalization Service in Baltimore, Maryland. It was six years after the Levensons had first filed the application for me to have legal status in the United States.

I was excited about the interview, yet as the time drew closer I became nervous. I couldn't help wondering if I was walking into a trap, but Laura assured me that the federal government could not employ deceptive practices.

The day finally arrived, and I took Melissa with me to the interview. It was a nail-biting experience. As an illegal alien, I had avoided the law for years, and the last person I wanted to encounter was an immigration officer. Yet there I was, walking into their building to tell them all about myself and how long I had been hiding from them.

Since I had all the required documents, the interview was brief. My application was approved, and I was issued a temporary green card that morning. In lieu of going to Colombia to pick up the permanent card, I had the option to pay a thousand-dollar penalty and have it mailed to me in Maryland. I paid the penalty because I was not taking any chances—I did not want to go to Bogota and get stuck there.

I could have skipped out of the INS building that day. The feeling was indescribable. Once I got on the interstate highway, I screamed, "Freedom!" Poor Melissa was startled and began to cry. Once she realized that everything was okay, she settled down and gave me a big smile.

It was a new beginning. I was free to go in and out of the country, and I no longer had a reason to panic at the sight of official vehicles in the neighborhood.

Illegal aliens learn to pick out official cars from a distance. An official vehicle pulling up in certain areas is reason enough for people to scale balconies and run. I no longer had to fear the INS.

Most importantly, I was no longer an "illegal alien." I had always found the term demeaning, but it was the official term, so that was what I was until that day. In one afternoon I went from illegal alien to lawful permanent resident.

I was not naïve to think that a green card would thrust doors open or make me wealthy; I still had to work hard and pursue new endeavors.

My first trip out of the country was to Montreal, to visit Alejandro. After the seven-year detour, it was good to finally see Canada. I liked Montreal, and I wondered how my life would have turned out if I hadn't stopped to see Esme in Virginia.

In December of that year, I went back to Colombia. The plane would not move fast enough for me. I landed in Bogota and caught a connecting flight to Pereira. It was good to be home.

I hadn't seen my younger brothers Diego and Juan Carlos in seven years, and I couldn't believe how much they'd grown. They still lived at home, and it didn't look like they would be moving out any time soon. That is not unusual in Colombia; people live at home till they get married or till they find a job in a different town. If neither event occurs, they can live in the family home for the rest of their lives.

My mother offered me all kinds of food, and a stream of neighbors poured in that afternoon and over the next few days. They brought me meals, wine, and fruits from their gardens. That was Colombian hospitality at its best. Even those who did not have much brought me gifts. In some cases, it was just a loaf of bread to welcome me back.

Not much had changed in the town. It had the same buildings and the same businesses. I went to the homes of old friends and discovered that most of them had left Pereira. The majority lived in the larger cities of Colombia, and a few were living in Spain, Canada, and the United States.

While I was happy to be in Colombia, I felt out of place. I missed Melissa and the rest of the Levenson family. When I called them, I talked about returning "home." The country which to me was once a strange land had become my home. I was now a visitor in the land of my birth.

I returned to the States three weeks later, and Melissa flew into my arms. Laura was off from work because she was having bodily aches. She was on pain medication, and I immediately noticed that she was taking the pills with alcohol. I scolded her, but she brushed me off.

I noticed things that I had not seen before. Laura was withdrawn, and her infectious laugh was gone. I detected other changes too. She was drinking more than usual. It was no longer just a bottle of beer in the evening; she drank vodka throughout the day. I wondered if the changes were recent or if they had been there for a while. Had I missed the signs because I was so close?

Laura slowly lost interest in everything and became distant. The kids were on their best behavior, and Josh was the model husband, yet none of that helped. We all had to make adjustments to accommodate the changes in her.

She started working from home, and that in my opinion did not help because it gave her the freedom to drink. She practically lived in the study and left the house only when she went to the liquor store or to doctors' appointments.

I cared about her, so I hid her liquor and threw it out when it was safe to do so. As fast as I hid the bottles, she replaced them. The recycling crew soon discovered that our bottles weren't always empty. They spent so much time going through our bins, I was afraid Laura would see them and realize what I had been doing.

I instituted an unspoken system. I put bottles containing alcohol in a plastic bag and placed it in the top left corner of the recycle bin. That eliminated the need to rummage through the bin. I probably caused those men to drink on the job, but better them than Laura.

Laura eventually stopped working altogether. Months turned into years, and the problem continued. Laura was sick, and we had a major problem on our hands. She was severely depressed, and the whole family suffered for it. Right before our eyes, she turned into someone we did not recognize. She was disconnected from the world and appeared to be engulfed by deep, dark sadness.

Laura suffered from panic attacks. One minute she wanted to flee from some invisible peril, and the next minute she would be paralyzed by unfounded fear. She was always tired, and even after sleeping for hours she would wake up fatigued. She seemed tortured, and the alcohol was clearly her way of numbing the pain.

Though the doctors found nothing physically wrong with her, she continued to complain about excruciating pain. She eventually had exploratory surgery on her arms and of course that meant more pain and more medication.

Josh and I tried to shield the children from the upheaval, and his parents stepped in to lend their support. The kids loved Grandpa and Grandma Levenson, and their presence certainly helped.

Laura's parents were divorced and lived in the Midwest. They visited a few times when Josh informed them of their daughter's condition. They struck me as pleasant people, yet, strangely enough, they did not have a close relationship with their daughter or her family.

Josh put Laura in rehabilitation programs. Some would help her for a while, but when you least expected it, she would relapse. She would start taking pain medication again, followed by periods of heavy drinking. She would disappear for hours, and more often than not, the police would call to let us know where she was.

She repeated the cycle so many times I lost count. It seemed like the better the preceding period of sobriety, the worse the depression that followed. After a while, we accepted Laura's situation as our new norm and dealt with her issues one day at a time. You never knew what she would do; you just knew something out of the ordinary would happen.

Chapter Fourteen

*Y*ou can always count on change when things are running smoothly. In the spring of 1998, Laura was doing much better, and the atmosphere in the house improved greatly. It was good to return to a quiet life.

My mother suffered a heart attack in June of that year. I wanted to visit her, but Laura too had a setback, and her family needed me. I had to rely on my sister Rosalinda for updates on our mother's condition.

That particular relapse was really bad, and it was hard to believe that Laura had been doing well just a few weeks earlier. She spiraled out of control, drinking vodka and popping pills all day. I had to put her undeniably frustrating needs before the needs of my own mother, and that was challenging.

It was an incredibly difficult time for my family, and Marcela almost drove me crazy. She was hysterical and blamed herself for not being there to take care of our mother. I also had to deal with my younger brothers who were still living at home yet refused to help Rosalinda. After a few nasty phone conversations, I decided that they were not worth the energy I was expending on them.

While our mother was still recovering, Rosalinda's sixteen-month-old grandson Emanuel became very ill. In addition to taking our mother back and forth to Bogota for treatment, Rosalinda had to help her daughter with the sick child. She did all of that while holding down a full-time job. My sister was shouldering a lot, and I was concerned about her health.

By August of that year, Emanuel was gravely ill. A battery of tests determined that the little boy had leukemia and was not expected to live.

I cried for three days and moped around the house till Josh snapped at me. "Why are you crying?" he demanded. "What good is that going to do?"

I gasped in disbelief. His words seemed incredibly harsh, and I had to retreat to my room to compose myself. When I returned, he asked what I was going to do to help the child. I was confounded. I had neither the expertise to offer professional advice nor the resources to send my nephew to renowned specialists. I didn't know what to make of the question.

Marcela fell apart when I told her the news. Although she had practically raised Margarita, she'd never met our niece's children. She was ready to pack her bags and return to Colombia.

Rosalinda and I had a hard time convincing Marcela not to leave. She was earning very little money, she was homesick, she still spoke very little English, and she was disenfranchised.

The thought of family members dying back in Colombia was too much for her.

Josh told me to get on the computer and look for help. For the next month or so, I searched the Internet while Melissa was at school. After I put her to bed at night, I was back at the computer till the early hours of the morning. I researched the illness, treatment, hospitals, and organizations that could help the child.

Efficient search engines make it much easier to find information today. Conducting research back then was often tedious.

I contacted the American Cancer Society and had the opportunity to speak to several doctors. While I conducted my research, I was constantly reminded of my abandoned dream of going to medical school. Had things gone my way, I would have been conferring with them as a fellow physician. It was no time to wallow in self-pity, so each time the thought crossed my mind, I directed my energy toward finding my nephew the help he needed.

The doctors agreed that the child needed a bone marrow transplant, and I had to find a hospital that was willing to take the case. I contacted three hospitals: Johns Hopkins Hospital in Baltimore, a hospital in Los Angeles, and the University of Alabama Hospital in Birmingham.

I was encouraged to hear that all three hospitals had experience in treating the illness. When they quoted the cost of treatment, I fell into despair. Treatment at Johns Hopkins was estimated at $480,000. The facility in California quoted $300,000, and the University of Alabama, Birmingham's estimate was $280,000. I didn't know how, but I knew I had to find money to pay for the transplant. I also had to find additional funds for visas, plane tickets, and lodging. It was overwhelming.

I did not let the language barrier get in my way—I wrote to as many organizations as I could find. During an online chat, I encountered a woman who recalled reading about a Colombian doctor who had lost his daughter to the same illness earlier that year. I searched for the doctor and ended up with a list of physicians with the same name. I gave the information to Margarita, and after many phone calls, she found the right one.

The physician told Margarita about the Colombian government's program for very sick children. The program, a well-kept secret, obligated the government to pay for a child's medical care abroad if adequate treatment was not available in Colombia.

He gave us a list of hospitals and organizations to contact, and it was reassuring to see that Johns Hopkins was on the list of hospitals he recommended. Lastly, he told Margarita how to get Emanuel to the United States on humanitarian grounds. He thought if we worked quickly, my nephew would have a chance at survival.

When Margarita asked her son's doctors why they did not tell her about the program, they said it was because he had only a two percent chance of survival. She was livid and demanded that the Colombian government pay for his treatment. Officials from the Ministry of Health stalled and frustrated her. She had to sue the government to get the child into the program.

The Colombian government pledged $250,000 toward the boy's treatment and made it abundantly clear that they would not give a penny more. Even with the least expensive option, we had to find an additional $100,000 for associated expenses.

I contacted charitable organizations for donations, and someone created a website to help us raise money online. I informed Johns Hopkins that we had some of the money, but they wouldn't perform the bone marrow transplant until we had $480,000 in hand. They did however contact other hospitals on our behalf. They negotiated with the hospital in Alabama (UAB) and offered to do the preliminary testing if UAB would accept the amount the Colombian government pledged. UAB agreed to perform the transplant under those terms.

Chapter Fifteen

Once we figured out how to pay for the transplant, we had to find bone marrow donors to be tested. Treatment could begin only after we found a match. Since the family was still in Colombia, testing was a challenge.

The team at Johns Hopkins University was willing to give me a kit to collect samples. The caveat was that once I received the kit, I had to get it to Colombia and back to the hospital in Baltimore within twenty-four hours. I could have thrown in the towel at that point, but by then I was galvanized. I was prepared to deal with any and all challenges and setbacks.

I coordinated with Margarita to make sure we were all on the same page. On the appointed date, I picked up the kit and handed it to a courier. I prayed while I counted down the six hours it took to get the kit from the Baltimore Washington International Airport to the El Dorado Airport in Bogota.

A medical team was at the airport with the family when the kit arrived. They quickly drew blood from Margarita, her husband José, and their two sons. Within an hour and a half of the kit arriving in Colombia it was onboard another flight en route to Baltimore.

Mobile phones were uncommon and reception was sporadic, so I could not get up-to-the-minute information from Margarita. Finding out the exact location of a package was out of the question, so I had a long, agonizing wait.

The blood specimens arrived at Johns Hopkins Hospital the following day. I was there, pacing the floor. I practically snatched the kit from the courier and ran. After handing it over, I collapsed onto a chair and stayed there for about an hour. We'd barely made the deadline. Another 20 minutes and our efforts would have been in vain.

It took three days to get the test results, and I cannot describe my level of anxiety. Every time the phone rang I went into a panic. To keep from going insane, I intensified my efforts to raise funds.

The call finally came. Emanuel's older brother Carmilo was a perfect match. I laughed and cried at the same time.

The hospital gave me a timeline during which treatment had to begin. We were almost out of time, and we did not have enough money. I went to several churches and pleaded my case. Most of them did not have the resources to help non-members. Two churches pledged to help when the family arrived in the United States, and a few pastors invited me to speak directly to their congregations.

It was a humbling experience to beg for money. A few people gave, many looked away, and others stared at me as though I had horns. The stares and dirty looks did not deter me. A life depended on my efforts, and I could not let my pride get in the way.

Immigrants are a tenacious group of people. It takes a certain mindset for a person to leave home and family and move to another country. Enduring hardship only increases resolve and builds thick skin.

I contacted St. Anthony's Catholic Church in Falls Church, where a priest ran a program for sick children. I was invited to meet the priest who was in charge of the Pan y Vino (Bread and Wine) charity. He helped me immensely and gave me the opportunity to address his congregation after Sunday mass.

A parishioner offered to help pay for the visas and airline tickets to get Margarita and her family to the United States. Her name was Carmen, and she was my guardian angel during that difficult time.

Carmen was an attorney who knew people in all the right places. She helped me raise funds from several churches and organizations. She also gave us contact information for a friend of hers at the US Embassy in Bogota.

My niece contacted that official, and within days she and her family obtained humanitarian visas to enter the United States. They didn't have to travel to Bogota and stand in long lines at the embassy; they simply mailed in their passports.

The days went by quickly, and on December 1st of that year, Margarita and her family arrived in Birmingham. It was three and a half months after I first received news of the baby's diagnosis.

I was at the airport to meet them. The little boy was frail, and his parents were drained. While Margarita and José were relieved to have cleared the first few hurdles, they were still very anxious about the days ahead.

From the airport, I took the family to a Ronald McDonald House near the hospital and helped them settle into their comfortable quarters. A Presbyterian church in Falls Church had raised money to pay for the family's accommodations at the facility.

The same church paid for transportation to and from the hospital, and a van arrived the very next morning to take the little boy to his first appointment. I served as a translator of sorts, since Margarita and José spoke no English.

The team at Johns Hopkins had been diligent in providing UAB with all the information they had compiled. The two brothers went through a battery of tests, and Emanuel was placed on medication. The transplant was scheduled for December 14th.

I had to get back home to the Levensons, so I left three days after the family arrived. The little boy was in good hands, and all I could do at that point was to pray that the transplant would be successful.

Arabelle:

I had a window seat on the flight back to Washington. I pressed my face against the glass and offered prayers of thanksgiving for what we had been able to achieve. I knew that without God pointing us in the right direction, the little boy would have died.

Chapter Sixteen

*I*t was late when I got home from Birmingham, so I was surprised to see that Melissa was still awake. She was thrilled to see me and flew into my arms. I lifted her up and twirled her around. She liked that and squealed with delight. Even though she was eight years old, she was fairly small, and I could still pick her up easily.

The rest of the family welcomed me home, but Laura barely said a word to me. After I put Melissa to sleep, I was ready to take a hot shower and climb into bed. I was emotionally spent, and I was looking forward to a good night's sleep.

Laura called me to the living room and calmly informed me that she no longer needed my services. I stared at her in disbelief; I was unable to speak. She said I had to leave because her daughter had become too attached to me. It sounded like an accusation of wrongdoing, and her words both stunned and hurt me.

Shortly after Melissa turned five, Laura had hinted that they would not be needing me for much longer. After raising the subject a few times, she'd dropped it and had not brought it up in years. That night however, I knew she meant it.

The Levensons were not just my employers, they had become my family. The idea of finding another job and a place to live was daunting. There was no guarantee that my next employers would be as kind.

I don't know how I got back to my room that night. I sat on the bed and stared at the walls. I tried to make a list of all the things I had to do before moving out, but I couldn't. I eventually fell asleep from exhaustion.

The next morning, Laura told me that I had until August of the following year to find a job and a new home. I was thankful that she gave me enough time to prepare.

I called my friend Yolanda and lamented to her. She explained that it was normal for nannies to feel dejected when their services were no longer needed. I resolved to do my best by the family till the very last day. I knew that even after I left I would stay close to them. They would always be near and dear to me.

Josh did not mention Laura's decision to let me go. He probably didn't agree with her yet chose to be silent. As much as possible, he refrained from arguing with her or agitating her. That was his way of keeping the peace and maintaining normalcy for his children.

When I told Marcela that we had to move, she went into a panic. Anyone would have thought that I heralded the end of time. The prospect of helping me pay for an apartment terrified her. She came home that weekend and stayed out of sight.

She didn't want to aggravate Laura in any way because the last thing we wanted was for her to put us out immediately.

Marcela and I sat in my room and cried. I happened to catch our reflection in the mirror, and we looked quite pitiful. I vowed never again to get attached to another family.

It was a very tumultuous time for Marcela and me. Not only were we being kicked out of the place we called home, there were other problems within our family. The date for the bone marrow transplant was fast approaching, and we were on edge. My mother wasn't doing well, and Rosalinda was having a hard time with our brothers at home. She also believed that her boss was trying to get rid of her.

When we called Margarita, she could tell that something was wrong on our end. She had enough worries of her own, so we didn't tell her about our predicament. Her son's immune system was severely compromised, and his doctors told her that unless they could raise his white blood cell count, they would have to postpone the transplant. In the interim, the little boy was running out of time.

We prayed for Margarita and her family that night. We also prayed for Laura and her family. We prayed for our mother and asked God to protect Rosalinda. Lastly, we asked for a safe and affordable place of our own. By the time we finished praying, I was worn out.

The transplant was postponed for a few days while the doctors tried to use diet and medication to boost Emanuel's white blood cell count. A Peruvian doctor who practiced holistic medicine told Margarita to give Emanuel foods rich in vitamin C and zinc. He also told us to give him yogurt and garlic. At that point, we were prepared to try anything. The boy could not hold down any food, and he grew increasingly weak. Something eventually worked; the white blood cell count increased, and the doctors were able to perform the surgery. I was frantic by the time it was done. The operation was a success, and both boys did relatively well.

A few days after surgery, Emanuel developed an infection and had to be hospitalized for a few weeks. Margarita, my sisters, and my mother were very discouraged. I was constantly on the phone trying to assure them that in spite of the infection, the little boy could still be cured. We were all very relieved when he was finally discharged.

Emanuel's recovery was slow, and the family's time at the Ronald McDonald House was almost up when doctors informed them that he would need extended follow-up visits. That meant they could not return to Colombia for a while. It also meant that they needed another place to live till Emanuel's treatment was complete.

I was trying to save for a place of my own, and I knew that renting an apartment for them would take a large chunk out of my savings. I sat on the floor and cried for a long time. I knew that when the time came, I would hand over the money and suffer for it later. I wanted to run away from everyone and everything, but I had no place to escape to.

One afternoon while the family was still at the Ronald McDonald House, they decided to take a long walk and explore the surroundings. They lost their bearings and asked a lady for directions. The lady spoke a little Spanish and befriended them. Her name was Janice, and she turned out to be a blessing.

Janice checked on Margarita and her family frequently and took them sightseeing around Birmingham. When she heard that they were looking for a place to stay, she introduced them to an affluent family. The family was touched by Margarita's story and offered her their basement, free of charge.

It turned out that the home was a mansion, and the basement was not the average basement; it was a luxurious apartment with a separate entrance. I was relieved when Margarita and her family moved in. Janice stayed close and continued to help them until they returned to Colombia seven months later.

Chapter Seventeen

I carried out my duties around the Levenson home as I counted down the months. I searched for a job and a new home. I hugged Melissa a little tighter each day; I didn't know if she would get the same level of attention when I was gone. I tried to steer her toward her mother, but that was an exercise in futility. I would seat Melissa beside Laura and ask her to draw pictures for her mother. Within minutes, either the mother would get up and leave the room or the child would come looking for me.

Laura had become even more distant and spent most of her time alone, drinking vodka. I tried to talk to her, but she became increasingly impatient with me. I realized that if I continued to aggravate her, she could fire me, so I backed off. It was heartbreaking to watch a loving wife and mother turn into a stranger that none of us could relate to. The brilliant mind had seemingly seeped out of what had become a hollow shell.

She disappeared frequently, and she gave us a scare when she left home one morning and did not return. We called everyone we could think of, and then we called the police and surrounding hospitals. A maid found her the next day in a hotel room where she'd apparently overdosed on pills and alcohol. Josh took her straight from the hospital to a rehabilitation center and continued to seek help for her. The man was often so weary I feared for his well-being.

I scoured the newspapers each day for job openings. I no longer wanted to work as a nanny. My nephew's illness forced me to communicate in English and at a level I had never anticipated. That coupled with the clerical experience I gained from working at the law firm, gave me the confidence to look for an entry-level position in corporate America.

I also looked at apartments, and I was alarmed at the rates. I knew I could not afford anything near the Levensons, but I thought I would find a decent place within a ten mile radius.

Apartments in my price range were located clear across town and in neighborhoods that I did not consider safe. As time went by, I became very worried. I couldn't find a job or a safe place to live.

I was going through the *Washington Post* in April of 1999 when an advertisement caught my eye. There were condominiums for sale in the downtown area of Silver Spring. I had previously looked at apartments in Silver Spring and had concluded that I could not afford to rent in that area.

A quick calculation showed that the mortgage on a one-bedroom condo would be less than the rent for an apartment in the same area. I didn't have much money, yet I dared to dream. I made an appointment to speak to the listing agent.

The agent was very helpful, and she explained the different programs available to first-time home buyers. To qualify for a loan, I had to have funds for a down payment and for closing costs. Fortunately, I had money in my bank account that belonged to Alberto. Back then, he frequently sent me money to purchase and ship vintage cars to him in Finland. The last deal had fallen through, and I was holding onto the funds. That made my bank statement healthy, and I was pre-qualified for a $65,000 loan.

There were thirteen listings, and we looked at all but one of the properties. That unit was in an ideal location, and it was priced within my range, so I insisted on seeing it. It was walking distance from the train station, five minutes from the beltway, and twenty minutes from downtown Washington. We went to that condo three times, and each time the tenant refused to let us in.

It wasn't until August that the owner bypassed the tenant and gave as a tour of the unit. The minute I walked into the condo, I was sold. I asked my agent to make an offer immediately. We offered $6,000 less than the asking price, and the seller countered with an additional $500. I accepted the counter-offer right away. I wasn't taking any chances on someone else offering full price.

We agreed on a settlement date of September 17th though I could not move in until November of that year. The owner had to give the tenant time to move out, and I had no objections whatsoever. I had not yet found a job, and I was not ready to pay the mortgage.

My mother screamed when I told her about the condominium. She was usually very restrained, so it was good to hear her sound excited. She was proud of me and told everyone in her neighborhood. Marcela was thrilled to hear that she would have a home to come to.

While I was happy about the condo, there was a small nagging voice that constantly reminded me that I needed a job to pay for it. I intensified the search and interviewed with several companies. In most of my interviews, I was given all of five minutes. The interviewers were not interested in hiring me.

A lot has changed since then. Today, Latinos are in offices, hospitals, schools, and everywhere else. Not too long ago, we were stereotyped and certainly not considered for office jobs. Latina women were supposed to be nannies, maids, cleaners, and bakers. To get into the corporate world, you had to know someone.

Chapter Eighteen

Toward the end of August, I attended an open house hosted by a subsidiary of US Airways. I applied for a position in customer service at the Washington Dulles International Airport, and I highlighted my bilingual skills.

I got the job, and it gave me an incredible sense of accomplishment. The benefits were phenomenal. I could fly anywhere on the airline for free, and I could fly on other carriers for a fraction of the fare. Better yet, the same benefits were extended to parents, spouses, and dependents of all employees. I could go back home to Colombia, and my mother could visit me.

I thought leaving the Levensons would disrupt my world. Instead, it changed my life for the better. Less than a year after I received notice from Laura, I purchased a condo, landed a job, and had unlimited opportunity to see the world.

My orientation at Dulles began on September 10th, 1999. My excitement turned into anxiety, and I barely slept the night before. Laura let me use their minivan, and I set off much earlier than I needed to. Finding the employee parking lot was a challenge, and I arrived in the terminal frazzled.

The trainer herded the twenty-two new hires around and showed us how to navigate the airport. We got our badges and took a tour of the terminals and the ramp.

We were recruited for the commuter division, and the trainer took us to meet the staff and observe them at work. It was a fast-moving operation, nothing like what I experienced with Avianca in Pereira. In fact, it was more like a bustling marketplace in Colombia. I was happy to see that the other new hires were as bewildered as I was.

I was intimidated, and I didn't know if I could work under that kind of pressure. More than anything else, the idea of making announcements over the loudspeaker terrified me. I was still very conscious of my accent. Since I didn't have alternatives, I had to steel myself against those fears.

To keep the job, I first had to survive a two-week new-hire training program. There was a lot to learn. We learned about the airline's computer system, city codes, safety procedures, aircraft types, and federal aviation regulations.

We took a test at the start of each day, and we could not answer more than a combined total of twenty questions incorrectly. Anyone who exceeded that number was promptly escorted out of the terminal. I was shocked at the number of trainees who dropped out within the first three days.

My settlement date happened to fall during the second week of training. I didn't want to make a bad impression by leaving class, yet I was anxious to make the condominium mine.

Fortunately, I hadn't missed many points on the tests, and I was in no danger of failing the class. Another trainee had a doctor's appointment, so we approached the trainer together and asked to be excused from class. The trainer was accommodating and allowed us to leave.

Settlement was an experience! I signed so many documents; my signature changed at least three times before we were done. When I received the key to the condo, I trembled uncontrollably and tears flowed down my cheeks. Both my realtor and the seller were puzzled.

I had flashbacks of my belongings strewn across the front of Esme's house. I pushed those thoughts out of my mind. I had a place of my own, and as long as I paid my mortgage, no one could throw me out.

The Levensons were thrilled to hear that I had closed the deal on the condominium. Even Laura congratulated me and agreed to let us stay till the tenant moved out. Having to leave Melissa was the only thing that dampened my spirits.

That night, I thanked God for giving me a place of my own. I prayed for the nanny in the Argentine household and for all those who endure hardship just to have a place to lay their head at night.

I was back at the airport the next morning and successfully completed the training program. Of the twenty-two new hires, only ten of us survived the program. I was especially proud of myself because many of those who failed spoke fluent English.

I began working at the gate the following week. It was organized chaos. I was stressed out and constantly felt dizzy. There were many moving parts, and we had to carefully orchestrate our efforts to make sure there were no mishaps.

We were under immense pressure to meet scheduled arrival and departure times. We also had the unusual situation of having to board multiple flights simultaneously and out of a single gate. The airline had expanded rapidly at Dulles Airport and had outgrown its existing infrastructure. There were barely enough gates for the larger planes, so the newly added commuter division was allocated only one gate through which to operate.

Departing passengers headed for various destinations were taken through the same doorway and down a flight of stairs to buses. Agents had to ensure that they handed passengers and paperwork to the right bus driver. Drivers had to make sure they went to the right aircraft. One small mistake had the potential to cause major delays and ripple effects.

In spite of the many announcements we made, passengers managed to get in the wrong lines, on the wrong buses, on the wrong aircraft, and to the wrong destinations. It was a nightmare.

As if that wasn't confusing enough, arriving passengers were bused to the terminal and came up the same staircase and through the same door. Every now and then some of those passengers would turn around and join departing passengers. It is unbelievable what intelligent people will do when they are out of their comfort zone.

It was hard to keep up with the pace, and there were times when I thought I would literally pull my hair out. I was especially nervous when I had to put unaccompanied minors or human organs on flights. Mishaps with either category usually had severe consequences, including termination of employment.

Four of us new agents bonded and we helped each other survive the first few days. I slowly got a hang of the job. When the time came to make my first announcement, I was nervous. Though my voice trembled, I somehow managed to get through it.

Once the senior agents realized we were there to stay, they accepted us as part of the family. We were a small part of the airline's overall operation at Dulles. Our team comprised college students, women in their thirties and older, and a handful of young men. We also had a group of policemen and firefighters who worked part-time.

It was my first time working with different ethnicities, and I was impressed by the diversity. I learned a lot about other cultures from my co-workers and from passengers. The Japanese carrier ANA's gate was right next to ours, and the Asian passengers intrigued me. They often travelled in large groups; they were organized and always had a sense of urgency.

Chapter Eighteen

Across the hall from us was the Austrian Airlines gate. As with ANA, their agents and crew members were always professional and did everything in orderly fashion. Next to them, we were a motley crew rushing around and trying to make sense of the madness.

Chapter Nineteen

I officially moved out of the Levensons' home in November of that year. Laura and Josh were very generous and gave me all the furniture I needed. They also gave me their minivan. Grandpa and Grandma Levenson gave me gifts and thanked me for all I had done for their family.

When the furniture arrived, it instantly transformed the condo into a home. I sank onto my knees and thanked God for my blessings. I had a job that came with great fringe benefits, and I had a home.

I spent the holiday season with the Levensons, and I was surprised to find that all the Hanukkah gifts were for me. They gave me kitchen appliances, linens, lamps, and practically everything else I needed. Marcela was thrilled to come home to a fully furnished condo. She was especially thankful that the mortgage was modest and I could afford to pay it without her help.

Every time I drove to work and saw the mountains in the distance, I felt a sense of freedom. The idea that I could get on a plane and soar above them was empowering. I no longer felt trapped in a land I could not leave. I had my green card, and I had the means to see the world.

My first trip on the airline was to Montreal, to visit Alejandro and his family. After that, I went to Miami for lunch and took overnight trips to Bermuda, Saint Thomas, and San Juan. I paid the nominal fee and upgraded my seat whenever possible. It was good to fly first class.

After a couple of months on the job, I ventured to work in Operations. I learned to handle ground-to-air communications. It was initially stressful, but after a few days I began to enjoy my role. The Colombian who was nervous about making announcements over the loudspeaker could be heard on aircraft and on radios throughout the terminals.

I invited Gladys and Yolanda to my home, and I shared my successes with them. Gladys took pleasure in telling Esme and Antonio about my green card, the condo, and the job that allowed me to go to Colombia as often as I pleased. To hear Gladys tell it, Antonio was visibly annoyed to hear about my good fortune and stormed out of the room.

They were still renting the little house in Falls Church, and they had a second child. Esme confided in Gladys that Antonio was drinking heavily. She had to support the family and was working three jobs to make ends meet. She still wanted to go back home, but after paying her bills and feeding her kids, there was no money left.

Esme wanted me to call her, and at Gladys' urging, I did. She apologized profusely for what her husband had done to me. She congratulated me on my achievements and was amazed that I had done so much as a single woman, and a Latina at that. She talked about going home and expressed her concerns that she had no skills to make a living. I reminded her that she was an intelligent woman who, with her family's support, could survive in Pereira. She was so dejected; I could not convince her that she could turn things around.

When I told her that I had gone back home a few times, she broke down and sobbed. She hadn't been back since she left, and she was beginning to despair that she would never set foot in Colombia again. By the end of the conversation, I needed a drink.

In retrospect, her husband did me a favor. When he threw me out of their house, I was forced to spread my wings and soar outside of their small world.

I could have been trapped like most Hispanic immigrants: stuck in the same job for years with no progress or prospects of becoming a legal resident. I could have been working for Hispanic bosses and earning low wages, with a constant threat of deportation over my head.

I could have married the first man that offered some security. That is how so many Latina women end up in abusive relationships with no way out. They plough through arduous lives, one day at a time. They have nothing to aspire to in the States and nothing to return home to. They have one baby after another and entrench themselves deeper into bad marriages.

Knowing the plight of others, I considered myself blessed and, above all, free. I continued to work at the airline, and I travelled when I could, sometimes with co-workers and sometimes on my own. I saw different parts of the United States, and I appreciated the vastness of the country and the efforts that had gone into making it a great nation.

I took Melissa to Finland, Colombia, France, and Spain. I used to think my chances of travelling had died with my dreams of becoming a physician, but with my job, I could see the world and I did not need much money to do so. God has a way of granting us our hearts' desires. He may not always use the avenues we prefer, yet the end result can be the same or even better.

When I was not travelling on my days off, I spent time with Laura and Melissa. Melissa was always happy to see me, but her mother was usually withdrawn.

Things were quiet until the end of the year, when Emanuel developed complications from his transplant. The family had to return to the hospital in Birmingham. Paying for his care was a lot easier the second time around. Significant donations had been made to his medical fund, and we were able to pay for his treatment and the family's expenses.

Right after Margarita and her family arrived in Birmingham, Rosalinda was forced to resign from her job. She took the opportunity to join her daughter. They found a place to live, enrolled the kids in school, and slowly settled in what was to become their new home.

Chapter Twenty

*I*n April of 2001, I became a citizen of the United States. I felt an unparalleled sense of security. I had always feared that a politician would someday change the rules and the green card would no longer guarantee permanent residence. Citizenship gave me the assurance that if something happened to me anywhere in the world, I could go to a US embassy for help.

I applied for a US passport, and when it arrived I clutched it for a good while. I finally had the coveted book that would allow me to enter many countries without a visa.

The passport prompted me to travel all over the world with co-workers. I was no longer intimidated by immigration officers in the States or in other countries. Customs and immigration officers everywhere asked fewer questions and seemed a lot friendlier. It was as though the US passport put a stamp of approval on my forehead, one that said "fit to enter."

That summer, almost two years after I started working at Dulles Airport, the airline shut down the commuter station and moved the operation to Ronald Reagan Washington National Airport. We were devastated. We had a good group of agents, a great management team, and we loved our station. National Airport had a much larger operation and an even faster-paced one. Many of us had flown in and out of that airport, and we knew the agents were not as friendly as our team was.

Except for the college students, everyone transferred to National, so that was comforting. We were still in for a culture shock. Their organization was different, and it took major adjustments on our part to fit in.

The first few days of integration were very awkward because the company did nothing to foster good relations between the two teams. We weren't formally introduced, and our new co-workers were standoffish. They looked right through us, and they stood by and watched us fail at many tasks.

The work ethic was starkly different from what we had at Dulles. Whereas we believed in teamwork, agents at National generally worked individualistically. The supervisors made things worse because they allowed their friends to congregate around them when they were supposed to be working.

The demographics of agents at National Airport were different from that of Dulles. Proximity to Washington DC resulted in a large number of inner-city youth, and the culture was very different. I grew up in a relatively small town, so I was not used to the bold ways of city kids in Colombia, let alone the urban youth of Washington DC. Their language was often colorful, and I was thankful that I did not understand most of the slang they used.

Some of them were abrasive and acted like schoolyard bullies. They ordered us about and tried to intimidate us. It took a lot of bickering—and, for some, tears—to fit into our new station. Strangely enough, some agents could be rude one day and then ask us for money the next day. Some would actually miss work when no one loaned them money for transportation.

I made the same hourly rate as they did, yet I never borrowed from anyone. I lived within my means. I wrote down all my expenses in a notebook, and at the end of each month I reviewed my budget to see where I could do better. After I paid my bills and bought food, I put the little I had left over in savings. I cooked my meals and packed my lunch each day. Only on rare occasions did I buy food at the airport. I still drove the old minivan the Levensons gave me, even though it had over two hundred thousand miles on it. With regular maintenance, it took me back and forth to work.

There were a few other Latinos who worked at the station, and we gravitated toward each other. We were called Mexicans and dubbed the Spanish Mafia. As far as some of my co-workers were concerned, everyone south of the border was Mexican and illiterate. They did not understand the nuances of our lives. As large a continent as South America is, they made no distinction between the countries or the people. They were certainly not aware of the existence of Central America.

I don't like being lumped together with every Latino as a Mexican. With their history and rich culture, I am sure Mexicans are just as resentful about being bundled with all Central and South Americans. People don't even realize that Mexico is in North America and not South America.

Considering the stringent curriculum in Colombia, I am certainly not illiterate, so I hated the notion that everyone from Latin America was an uneducated peasant. I thought I would be remiss if I said nothing, and that led to many altercations on the job.

When I pointed out that I was Colombian and not Mexican, it only made things worse. I was subjected to crude jokes, and if there is one thing that makes me furious, it is derogatory blanket statements about Colombians.

In many minds, Colombia is synonymous with cartels and cocaine. The truth is that the average Colombian is weary of the drug trade and has suffered from it in one way or another.

I would go into tirades and tell anyone within earshot of the great country, its accomplished people, rich heritage, and natural beauty. God was creative in designing my motherland, and it bothered me that people were oblivious to that.

Colombia has a lot to offer. It is a large and mountainous country with snow-capped mountains in the higher elevations and year-round sunshine in low-lying areas. In the west, the Sierra Nevada de Santa Marta Mountains rise majestically from the Pacific coastline and run north and across the country to the Caribbean Sea on the east coast.

Although both coasts boast hundreds of miles of beautiful beaches, they have contrasting terrain and sand. Beaches on the Pacific coast have black sand against deep blue water, with lush rainforests rising in the background. On the Caribbean coast, coconut palms line beaches which have mountains or bright orange desert as a backsplash. Waves from crystalline and turquoise waters of the Caribbean Sea lap at pearl-white or brown sands.

The country has a rich history, with churches, forts, and castles that date back to the 1500s. The Spaniards left us ancient cities and traditions. Colombians have built ultra-modern cities that thrive on technology and legitimate commerce.

Tourists marvel at the architecture and location of many of our buildings. A classic example is a cathedral known as Nuestra Señora de Las Lajas, or Our Lady of the Jewels. The cathedral is hewn from stone and suspended between two mountain slopes, with a waterfall as the backdrop.

Coca is not the only crop grown in Colombia. Our coffee ranks among the best in the world, and we are a leading producer of flowers. Exotic fruits native to Colombia are now sold in high-end supermarkets across the globe. Because of the rich volcanic soil, our produce is often three times the size of that found in other places. Unfortunately, the same land that yields these bumper crops also provides fertile fields to cultivate coca.

The more I tried to educate my co-workers, the more cruel the comments they made. They weren't interested in learning anything new, and desperately trying to tell them positive facts about Colombia only made me seem unhinged. They enjoyed taunting me, and in hindsight I gave them plenty of opportunity to do so.

After a while, I stopped trying to change their minds and left them to their ignorance. The only feather in the caps of some of those agents was the fact that they were American and spoke fluent English. With all the opportunities available to them, they'd accomplished very little.

After months of frustration on the job, I came to the realization that while I could not change my co-workers, I could adjust my attitude. I did my fair share of work and refrained from complaining about agents who did not pull their weight. That was still not enough, and the atmosphere remained toxic. When an agent threatened to slash my car tires, I considered quitting the job.

The young man had repeatedly been rude to me, and when I finally responded in kind, he was outraged that a Hispanic dared to stand up to him. He swore at me and, among other things, told me to go back to Mexico.

I thought I would be better off working with a smaller group of agents, so I volunteered to work in Operations. Things were just as bad, if not worse. The agents in Operations saw my presence as an intrusion; I was not one of them. My calls on the radio went unanswered, so I was unable to do my work effectively. All my appeals for intervention were ignored by supervisors and managers alike.

I eventually gave up the position in Operations and returned to the gate. The managers could not find a qualified agent to fill the vacancy, so they tried to strong-arm me into going back. When I refused to do so, the station manager threatened to fire me for insubordination. I had taken the initiative to learn that function on my own time, and I was not going to let anyone force me to work in the hostile environment. I did not give in.

Chapter Twenty-One

Less than three months after we moved to National Airport, the events of September 11th, 2001, occurred. I was boarding passengers on a flight when a pilot whispered in my ear that a plane had crashed into the World Trade Center. I assumed that it was an accident involving a small private plane, but I soon learned that it was a commercial jetliner. Although it wasn't one of our aircraft, the mood instantly became somber. Being part of the airline family, we mourn the loss of any carrier's flight.

As was to be expected, there was chatter and uneasiness among passengers. Before we could process the information, we heard that there was a second plane crash. We also heard that terrorists were responsible for the crashes. Like the rest of the world, we were in shock.

Some passengers gathered around television monitors in disbelief while others stood in line, clamoring for attention. We had hysterical passengers who demanded that we send their flights out immediately so they could get home to their families. Others demanded refunds or asked to be rebooked on future flights; the last thing they wanted to do that morning was to get on planes.

There was no directive from the airport authority, and neither the supervisors nor the managers had any guidance. The experience was unprecedented, and no one wanted to make the wrong call. We didn't know whether to continue working or bring the operation to a halt.

I went to Operations to see if they'd heard from the airport authority, dispatch, the tower or anyone up the chain of command. I got there just in time to hear breaking news that air traffic had been halted nationwide. The situation in Operations quickly deteriorated.

Incoming crew were clamoring for parking spots, outgoing planes wanted to return to the gates, and ground crew were screaming for guidance. Aircraft headed to other destinations were also calling in and pleading for clearance to divert to National Airport.

Every agent in Operations had a phone pressed to one ear and a radio in the other hand as they scrambled to answer calls and find parking spots for everyone. I never got a chance to ask if the agents had received any instructions on how to proceed.

Several calls came in about a low-flying aircraft, and then there was a string of inaudible transmissions followed by piercing screams and the screeching of radios. It sounded like a hundred flights calling in simultaneously. We couldn't tell what the pilots were saying, but we understood soon enough.

A couple of transmissions came through clearly, and pilots frantically reported that an aircraft had crashed into the Pentagon. Within seconds, ground crew radioed that debris and ash were falling on the ramp. The closed-circuit television showed smoke billowing across the north end of the airport.

There was total pandemonium. Hysteria filled the airways. Every pilot was anxious to land, and you could hear the fear in their voices. No one wanted to be diverted to another airport.

A television station reported that a plane had indeed been crashed into the Pentagon. Before we could recover from the shock, the reporter announced that a fourth hijacked plane was headed for Washington DC.

There was utter chaos in Operations. Every last one of the thirty phone lines was ringing. Expletives were flying, radios were screeching, pilots were screaming, and in the end no one could be heard.

Ground-communications agents yelled fruitlessly at ramp personnel to marshal planes in. Because of the ash and debris raining down on them, ramp agents were sheltering on buses and in tugs. Frustrated pilots randomly pulled onto gates and parking spots. They wanted to get off their aircraft!

It dawned on me that the airport was as good a target as any. I hurried to the locker room, grabbed my purse, and headed for the gates. I wanted to be in an area where I could at least run for safety.

A loud voice came over the public address system and ordered everyone to evacuate the terminals. Airport police began to escort passengers and employees out of the terminal. Those who worked in the commuter section first had to take buses to the ramp, to get our passengers off planes.

Thick black smoke continued to fill the sky, and ash fell on us as we went from one plane to the next. The airport authority opened a gate that I had never seen unlocked, and we took passengers directly to the front of the airport.

We joined evacuees from the terminals, and police officers led us down a side road. Hundreds of passengers and employees bumped into each other as they tried to hail cabs or ran to their cars.

A Bolivian co-worker had a panic attack, and I literally dragged her a mile and a half to the parking lot. I put her in my van and made arrangements to meet her mother in Maryland. With everyone trying to leave at the same time, it was horrendous. It took us forty minutes to get out of the airport and onto the George Washington Parkway.

As anxious as I was to leave the airport, not knowing what lay ahead was unsettling. Were the roads closed? Were there terrorists unleashing evil in the streets of Washington? Would I make it home safely? I had to be strong for the sake of my companion who was cowering in the front seat.

From the highway, I could see flames shooting out of the Pentagon. It was like a scene out of a violent movie. There were fire trucks, police cars, ambulances, and all manner of emergency-response vehicles there. There were also hundreds of people milling around the parking lots.

Drivers slowed down to get a better look. I on the other hand, drove as quickly as I could. I felt sick knowing that there had to be bodies burning in the fire. The traffic became heavier as we went along, and at times we barely moved. We came to a complete stop at the exit to the CIA facility. I thought I too would have a panic attack. I looked around furtively, wondering if the facility was a target. Mercifully, my companion had no idea where we were or what the agency did, otherwise she probably would have had a heart attack.

It took two hours to get to Bethesda, where I handed my co-worker over to her mother. When I finally made it home, I sat in front of the television and, like everyone else, tried to make sense of the carnage. I couldn't understand how man could do that to his fellow man. I certainly couldn't imagine what the families of the victims were going through. I knew many of our crew members and I would have been devastated if any of our planes were involved.

For the next few days, airports were closed nationwide. We waited for news on when we could return to work. Days turned into weeks, and long after all other airports reopened, ours remained closed.

Agitated airline employees held press conferences and appealed to the government to reopen the airport, but their efforts proved fruitless. Little did we know that it would be months before we returned to work.

Chapter Twenty-Two

I spent time with the Levensons during my time off from the airline. Laura was going through a very rough period, so her friend and neighbor Nancy stopped by daily to check on her.

I sometimes accompanied Nancy when she ran errands. I was with her when she went to a fancy assisted living facility to visit a lady who was 102 years old. Nancy didn't think the lady would let me enter her apartment, so I had to wait outside till she got permission to take me in.

The old woman peered at me curiously and said nothing when Nancy introduced me. Her name was Florence. She cocked her head and slowly looked me over from head to toe. I didn't know whether to sit or remain standing.

After a few seconds, Florence ordered me to sit down. Considering her age, her voice was pretty strong. She fired questions at me and seemed to transform when she learned that I was from Colombia. She spoke to me in Spanish and told me she'd spent several months in Bogota back in 1945.

She was animated when she recalled her time in Colombia, and she talked to me until she shut her eyes, seemingly tired. I sat quietly while I waited for Nancy to finish tidying up the old woman's bedroom.

"Why are you not at work?" Florence asked with her eyes still closed. I was startled, since I thought she was asleep. I explained how the events of September 11th had affected my job, and for a while she said nothing.

"Would you like to keep me company at night?" Florence asked me. It was a strange question. "I will pay you," she added quietly. She explained that her nurse left at six o'clock in the evenings and she was by herself till morning.

Her words tugged at my heart. In Colombia, it would be an abomination to let an elderly person live alone. Relatives take care of the elderly, and in the absence of family, neighbors step in.

I guess a culture that permits a parent to kick a child out at the age of eighteen, breeds children who can abandon parents and relatives when they are elderly and infirm. Florence must have read my mind because, unsolicited, she offered the explanation that she had no children and no family.

She said the closest she had to family was a woman she called her niece. She elaborated that they were not related; the woman was actually the niece of a deceased friend. The niece was married to a senator and lived a few miles away.

The information took me by surprise. Where I come from, it is rare to find an individual who has no family. At the very least they have distant relatives.

I felt sorry for the old lady and agreed to keep her company. A week later, I was working for her. I arrived at seven o'clock every evening and stayed till morning when her nurse arrived.

Florence and I bonded very quickly, and I felt as if I had been blessed with the gift of a grandmother. I always found her sitting directly behind her front door, waiting for me. As soon as I walked through the door, she would ask if the airport had been reopened. For two months, my answer was no.

Florence was a very accomplished woman. She'd founded and successfully run a patent office in Virginia for decades. She told me intriguing stories about her life, and she had many pictures to chronicle the adventures of her younger years.

Although Florence enjoyed doing things for herself, I soon noticed changes. She became more frail and was hospitalized at the end of November. That was when she told me that she had leukemia. She refused treatment and asked her doctors to send her home.

Nancy made arrangements with a hospice to ensure that all of Florence's needs were met. She also informed the niece that the old lady's condition was worsening.

I continued to spend my evenings with Florence. She had some good days where she was able to sit up and chat. She would tell me more stories about her life, and she wouldn't stop talking till she wore herself out and needed her oxygen tube. With no children, grandchildren, or great-grandchildren, she'd probably never had anyone she could tell her life story. In me she found someone who was interested, and she was eager to share as much as she could while she still had breath in her.

I was grateful for the opportunity to spend time with Florence. She paid me handsomely, and I knew it was God's timely intervention. He knew that Florence needed someone to love her, and I needed the money to pay my bills. I became so fond of the old lady that, had she told me she could no longer afford to pay me, I would still have kept her company.

On December 1st, 2001, I received the long-awaited call to return to work. I went in for orientation, and from there I went to Florence's apartment. The nurse let me in, and I went straight to the bedroom to tell her the good news. Florence had the biggest smile on her face when she saw me in uniform. "You are back at work!" she said as she hugged me excitedly.

She listened as I recounted all that happened at the airport that day. She was saddened to hear that the Bolivian girl who suffered a panic attack on September 11th had ended up in a mental institution.

After a while, she leaned back against the pillows, adjusted her oxygen tube, and told me to take a nap on the recliner in her room.

I smiled as I watched Florence sleep peacefully. I made my-self comfortable and shut my eyes to take a short nap. When I woke up, I was shocked to see that it was 2 a.m. An unfamiliar sound caught my attention, and it took me a few seconds to realize that it was the oxygen tank.

The air was leaving the tank and going nowhere. I jumped up, and in my haste I tripped over the leg of the recliner and fell. "Florence!" I called out as I scrambled to her bedside. Her eyes were open, yet she did not move.

The oxygen tank continued to hiss while I tried to compose myself. The nurse had instructed me to check Florence's feet if she became unresponsive on my watch. They were cold and blue. I pushed the call button and dropped to the floor.

A nurse arrived moments later. She checked Florence's vital signs and pronounced her dead. She shut the old lady's eyes, made a few calls, and methodically prepared her for pick up.

Although the woman was over a hundred years of age and had been deteriorating daily, her death took me by surprise. I had never been alone with a dead body, so I was traumatized to think that I had been sleeping just a few feet away from one.

I felt like I had failed Florence. I was right there when she slipped away, but I did not get the chance to hold her and pray with her in her final moments. To me, she died alone.

The undertakers arrived at dawn, and it broke my heart to watch them put the body in a bag. That scene put things in perspective for me. After a hundred and two years, the end had still come. Florence had drawn her last breath and left this world, relinquishing everything.

We work hard to acquire status and material things, and we are disappointed when we miss the mark. One fine day, we leave it all behind. All we get are one final outfit, one casket, and one grave.

I waited till morning to call Nancy. She immediately guessed that her friend had passed away. I offered words of comfort even though I was crying myself. She came to the apartment to begin burial arrangements.

Florence had written down her wishes and planned her funeral, step by step. She had even paid the funeral home for their services, chosen her casket, and paid for a grave. I wailed when Nancy read the list; the concept was foreign to me. In my culture, people are spared the morbid task of planning their own funeral.

Nancy called the so-called niece to inform her of Florence's demise and get her input on a date and time to hold the funeral. The woman was indifferent; she didn't intend to be there. Her response did not surprise Nancy. In all the years that she'd known Florence, the niece had only visited the old lady twice. Someone from her husband's office had been tasked with calling Florence from time to time.

Nancy called the funeral home and set a date. She notified Florence's attorney and the charity to which she had left her household items. She went through the closet and found the suit that the old lady had asked to be buried in. It had already been dry cleaned.

Nancy pressed the suit against her body for a few minutes. We sat in the bedroom and cried. Never again would we see that feisty little lady propped up in the bed. Never again would she return to her home.

On the day of the funeral, Nancy and I met Florence's nurse and a long-time friend of hers outside the building. A limousine arrived to pick us up, and right before we left, a young man showed up and rode with us to the church. He was the son of the senator's wife; his mother had delegated him to attend the funeral on her behalf.

The only other people at the church were the funeral director and his staff, the priest, and a small choir. It was a simple service, and the choir sang a few songs that Florence had selected. Nancy said a few words, but other than that, there was no tribute, no biography, and no family members to share fond memories.

I cried as though I'd known Florence all my life. I was sad that such an accomplished lady had only a handful of people at her funeral, none of them related to her.

In Colombia, the poorest of people have mourners at their funeral. Distant relatives, church members, neighbors, grandchildren of acquaintances, and even strangers show up. Standing in the church that day, I made a conscious decision not to end up like Florence.

The limousine was the solitary vehicle that followed the hearse to the cemetery. After the burial, Nancy, the nurse, and I went back to the apartment to pack up Florence's belongings. I was teary-eyed the whole time. The old lady's death impacted me a lot harder than I could ever have imagined. I had grown to love her.

Chapter Twenty-Three

Three days after the funeral, I received a call from Florence's attorney. I was surprised and certainly very grateful to hear that she had left me fifteen thousand dollars. She also left the nurse some money, and to the so-called niece she left millions of dollars. I wondered if the woman would have any remorse for not visiting Florence and not attending her funeral.

After watching Florence die a lonely old woman, I was convinced that I needed my own nuclear family. Though I loved Melissa dearly, I was acutely aware that she wasn't mine. I wanted children of my own, and I resolved to have at least one, be it biological or adoptive.

I also vowed that once I reached the age where I could no longer work, I would move back to Colombia. I wasn't going to grow old in the United States and be confined to an apartment by myself. I was definitely not going to stick around long enough to be committed to a nursing home.

For many years, my life revolved around Melissa, and I had done very little socializing. There was no man in my life, and I was apprehensive about venturing out to meet new people. I knew I had to get out more.

Esme's husband and a couple of chauvinistic guys in the area had soured me on Colombian men. Other Latino men whom I encountered seemed just as bad. Some were narcissistic and did not have much respect for women. What bothered me more than anything else was that many of them lacked the level of education I wanted in a man.

The educated Latinos in the States were looking for women with college degrees. Among Latin Americans, education sets a woman apart and is a determining factor in careers, marriage, and social standing.

With a degree, I would have had leverage; without it, the pickings were slim. It didn't matter that I had attended some of the best schools in Colombia and had two years of college education. I often wanted to kick myself for not completing my undergraduate studies.

Ironically, if I had stayed in Colombia, not having a degree would have had less of an impact on my life. I could still have been in the right circles by virtue of friends and classmates in high places. In the States, I was in a pool with all Latina women who did not have higher education.

That is one of the prices you pay for leaving home. Not only do you start at the bottom of the economic ladder, you could also end up at the bottom of the social ladder.

For the next couple of years, I dated casually. Even though I was eager to get married and start a family, settling for the first person who came along was out of the question. I wanted a man like my father, one that my children would be proud of.

More often than not, I didn't bother to call my suitors after the first date. They either lacked ambition or they'd been beaten down by the system and were content to live mundane lives. There were also those who were looking for a woman with a green card. It was so frustrating—I had to find things to do to keep my mind off my mission.

I focused on my English lessons and pushed myself to learn more about computers. I also read motivational books and took trips to different countries to see the sights and broaden my horizons. Every now and then, Laura accompanied me. Traveling seemed to help both of us immensely; we always came back rejuvenated.

Laura had been going through a relatively peaceful phase and became very excited when Melissa's thirteenth birthday drew near. She planned her daughter's bat mitzvah and threw herself into the preparations. She was eager to show everyone that she was on the road to recovery.

I shopped for Melissa's dress and selected a beautiful lavender outfit at Nordstrom. She loved the attention she got from everyone, and she conscientiously studied her passages from the Torah.

Laura invited two hundred family members and friends. Her parents flew in from the Midwest, and Josh's parents of course were there. Even my mother flew in from Pereira.

Melissa's dress fit perfectly, and she looked like a princess. She was so nervous; I thought she would be unable to stand up in front of the guests. Once she got up on the altar, she recited her passages in flawless Hebrew. I still tease her older brother and sister about making mistakes during their ceremonies.

A reception followed the bat mitzvah. The theme was travel, and each guest received a boarding pass with their seat assignment. The tables represented different countries, and the centerpieces were three-dimensional puzzles of landmarks in the respective capital cities. Big Ben, Jerusalem's Temple Mount, the Washington Monument, the Eiffel Tower, the Imperial Palace, the Kremlin, and the Colosseum were all featured.

The event was as lavish as a wedding, and my mother repeatedly told Marcela and me how much she loved grand affairs and how much she wanted to attend our weddings. I wanted that more than she could ever have imagined. There wasn't a day that went by without me thinking that I had to get married and start a family.

Two days after the bat mitzvah, my mother fell ill and had to be rushed to a hospital in Silver Spring. Though she didn't have health insurance, she was admitted because her condition was serious. Doctors believed that medication she had been taking for arthritis had caused a cardiac event.

My mom shared a room with an elderly woman who constantly soiled her bed. The smell was revolting. Marcela and I begged the nurses to move our mother into another room, but they ignored us. When we appealed to the doctors for help, they too did nothing.

Our mother refused to eat in the room and kept trying to climb out of bed. She finally had to be restrained. As painful and degrading an experience as it was, we didn't have the option to move her to another hospital.

Laura visited my mother three days after she was admitted. She threw a fit when she stepped into the room and threatened to sue the hospital. She sounded every bit like the powerful attorney she used to be.

The nurses apologized profusely, and within minutes my mother was moved to a private room where she remained for ten days. I learned a valuable lesson: some people can drive right through what to others might be an unyielding mountain.

After my mother's discharge from the hospital, we took care of her for a few weeks and sent her back to Colombia. The experience scared her so much; she vowed never to make any more trips outside the country.

I visited her a few months later to make sure she was okay, and she had changed drastically. She was forgetful, and she often didn't make any sense. I took her to see a specialist, and he said it was the onset of dementia.

It was depressing news for all of us, but Marcela was affected the most. Since our mother could no longer travel to the States, there was a possibility that they would never see each other again.

It was a tough situation. We didn't know how much longer our mother would have her memory, yet we were too far away to spend quality time with her. We called her often, hoping that would help keep her mind alert.

Chapter Twenty-Four

I had planned to travel to Finland with my mother in January of 2004. Since she couldn't go, I invited a co-worker to accompany me. Alberto and his wife took us on a ferry from Helsinki to Tallinn, Estonia. As we sat on deck enjoying the view, my co-worker talked fondly about her four children. My brother and his wife talked about their daughters. I didn't have much to contribute.

Uncharacteristically, I let on that the idea of having kids was weighing heavily on my mind. They all thought I would make a great mother, and they encouraged me to have a child. I lamented that since there was no special man in my life, marriage and kids were not in the foreseeable future.

While I harped on finding the right man, my co-worker raised the topic of single parenthood. She was American, so for her that was commonplace and acceptable. It was Alberto who shocked me when he chimed in and agreed with her. I was dumbfounded. Back in Colombia, it was taboo to have a child out of wedlock, so I couldn't believe my brother would entertain the idea.

Alberto reminded me that I no longer lived in Colombia. In his opinion, I had to do what was best for me and not worry about what family or society would say. He said I needed a child who would love me and have a duty to stand by me in my old age.

We discussed adoption and unconventional methods of conception. Just like that, I went from thinking that I had no options to realizing the possibilities.

I had briefly dated a decent guy who wanted a baby. He had been through a nasty divorce, so he was not interested in marriage. At the time, I felt insulted and stopped talking to him. I made a mental note to call him when we returned to Maryland. Of all the possibilities we discussed, I liked the option of co-parenting best.

The rest of the trip went by quickly, and I was happy to get home and start my research. I explored every one of the options we discussed in Finland. I had long debates with myself. Did I have the fortitude to withstand my family? Was it worth the fights that would take place? On the other hand, would the family be there when I was old and alone?

I decided that unless "Mr. Right" miraculously showed up and proposed, I was going to have a baby outside of marriage. It crossed my mind that my mother could have a heart attack, yet I was willing to risk it. She had ten children, so she could not begin to understand the emotions of a woman yearning for a child.

I believe that some women genuinely do not want children. Others come to terms with a condition that renders them incapable of having kids. A woman that is obsessed with becoming a mother will go to great lengths. She cannot worry about what others have to say; her desire outweighs all else. I was definitely in the last category.

I already had Alberto's support, and the only other sibling whose endorsement I needed was Eduardo. I looked up to him, and he was the person whose reaction I feared the most.

I expected Eduardo to go through the roof, but he didn't. He listened quietly as I explained my fear of being alone or feeling unfulfilled in my latter years. He asked me several questions, and when he was satisfied that I had given the matter plenty of thought, he told me I had his support. That meant a lot to me.

I tested the waters with Marcela. I told her that I planned to have a baby within a year, and she immediately asked who I was marrying. When I told her about my options, her jaw dropped, and she looked like she was going to faint. When she recovered from the shock, she lectured me on what society and religion expected of me. She completely ignored my argument that I was an adult with the right to decide what was best for me.

She told Rosalinda and our mother about my intentions, and they basically forbade me to have a baby out of wedlock. I knew there would be major battles, but at that point I was past caring.

I told my closest friends about my plans, though I did not disclose which method I had decided on. They were understanding and gave me their unconditional support.

Chapter Twenty-Five

*I*n April of 2004, I found out that I was pregnant. I was ecstatic—that is, until I had my first bout of morning sickness. I could never have imagined how bad it could be. There were times when I thought my insides would fall into the toilet bowl.

I had not anticipated that aspect of pregnancy, and I suddenly felt vulnerable. When I had to take a few days off from work, I began to second guess my decision to have a baby.

I told Eduardo and Alberto my dilemma, and they reminded me that there was no going back. I had to be strong and weather the storms ahead.

The Levensons were happy for me, and even Laura showed interest in my pregnancy. That gave me the courage to break the news to Marcela. She was melodramatic. I felt like a nun confessing her pregnancy to a Mother Superior.

Marcela alternated between throwing her hands up in despair and covering her face in shame. With her hands on her hips, she followed me all over the condo demanding answers.

"Ay Dios mio! Ay Dios mio!" she yelled in between questions. I half expected her to get on a broom and circle around me. If I hadn't been so nauseous, I might have found her actions comical.

Once she broke the news to the family, they were in uproar. Anyone would have thought that I'd killed a child. They demanded to know the father, and I refused to answer them. My mother and my sisters thought I had broken religious laws and every moral code. My brothers thought I had disgraced the family. They couldn't fathom the notion that I may have used alternative methods of conception; to them, that was anathema.

I was initially indifferent to their behavior; I was expecting it. The phone calls kept coming, and the comments were vicious. The cruel words cut deeper and deeper, and it got so bad that I finally stopped taking their calls. I only spoke to Eduardo and Alberto.

I continued to have a tough time with the pregnancy, and I suffered a miscarriage at the end of the second month. I sank into depression. I tried to talk myself into going on with my life, but that did not work.

I learned firsthand that depression occurs not only in the mind but also in the belly. I felt as though I had a stomach full of negatively charged energy. The slightest movement jarred my nerves to the point where I wanted to ball up in a corner and die.

Having witnessed Laura's battles, I knew what I was up against, and that almost drove me insane. I feared that I would never return to normal.

I had to keep working, and that turned out to be a blessing because it took my mind off my problem. Alberto and Eduardo were sympathetic and continued to be supportive. Eduardo wanted to visit me, but he had developed chronic back pain and was unable to fly. He was also going through a nasty divorce, and by all accounts, his wife was doing her best to fleece him.

The rest of the family offered me no condolences. After a few snide comments, they backed off, and I kept my distance. Their actions hurt me and made me more determined to try again. I needed a child who would love me unconditionally.

By the fall of that same year, I was pregnant again. Alberto was excited for me. When I called to tell Eduardo, he was quite ill. His backaches had worsened, and he could barely move. His divorce was finalized, and he'd walked away with his clothes and nothing else.

I kept my pregnancy quiet, but with time Marcela noticed. She was horrified. Before she could get sanctimonious all over again, I put her in her place. I made it very clear that I was not going to allow her to harass me in my own home. That silenced her, and I did not see her for months. When she did come by, I knew it was just so she could go back and report her findings to her mother and her siblings.

Rosalinda called from Alabama to offer her unsolicited opinion, and I immediately hung up on her. As for the rest of the family, I simply avoided them. My need to fill a void in my life was inconsequential to them. They cared more about what neighbors in Pereira would say.

When I was five months pregnant, Eduardo was diagnosed with cancer of the kidney. I did not have the strength or the drive to conduct research on treatment like I did for Margarita's son Emanuel. Eduardo assured me that his ex-wife was doing all she could to get him the best care possible. Given the acrimonious divorce, I found it strange that she was helping him.

Eduardo had surgery to remove his left kidney, and then he went through chemotherapy. The treatment took its toll on him, and he struggled physically. I would have loved to visit him, but in order not to jeopardize my pregnancy, I had stopped flying. I called him as often as I could afford to.

The last month of my pregnancy was tiring. I worked till the fortieth week, and it took every effort to get out of bed in the mornings. My friends threw a baby shower and gave me the cutest little clothes and toys for my baby. Especially since most of my family wanted nothing to do with me, I was thankful that I had good friends.

I started maternity leave on a Friday, and Eduardo's daughter Miriam flew in that Sunday. We went shopping for a few last-minute items, and I waddled from store to store, guzzling bottles of water and making frequent trips to the restroom.

I was exhausted by the time we got home. After I showered and climbed into bed, I felt the need to go to the bathroom yet again. Lowering myself onto the toilet seat was a challenge. I dozed off for a few seconds, and when I woke up, I realized something was different. I felt like I was emptying a barrel of water.

I called out to Miriam who instinctively phoned her mother. When she relayed the message that my water had broken, I sat on the toilet, trembling. After all the literature I'd read and the conversations I'd had with my doctor, I was still not prepared for that moment.

My doctor had planned to induce labor the very next day, and that orderly process was what I was mentally prepared for. The baby had other plans, and by three o'clock in the morning we were on our way to the hospital.

The contractions were initially painful yet tolerable. I wanted to experience childbirth the natural way, so I refused the epidural. At least that was what I told the anesthesiologist. Three hours later, I was singing a different tune.

The pain was so intense I thought my eyeballs would literally fall out of my head. My blood pressure rose steadily, and I felt exhausted and disoriented. I begged for medication.

Even after I got the epidural, I felt a lot of discomfort. I wanted to get up and leave; I did not want to be a part of the ordeal. Right there in that delivery room, I questioned my judgment.

Chapter Twenty-Six

My baby boy was born at 11:12 a.m. on April 29th 2005, and I was overjoyed at meeting the precious little fellow. Any doubts or regrets I may have had during labor dissipated quickly. I didn't know I had the capacity to love anyone as much as I loved my son.

I was thankful for the safe delivery and for a healthy baby. However, the logistics of taking care of a child became crystal clear, and I was terrified that I would not live up to my responsibility.

I called the Levensons, and they rushed to the hospital to meet the newest member of the family. My co-workers also visited, and I was touched by the way they cared about my son and me.

I named my baby Leon and asked Miriam to be his godmother. Leon and I were discharged the next morning, and I tried to settle into my new role. Within twenty-four hours, I was sleep deprived. Leon was like an overly efficient alarm clock; he woke me up every two hours.

Three days after delivery, I blew up like a balloon and had to be hospitalized. Miriam took care of Leon while I was away, and although I missed my baby, the uninterrupted sleep made the separation worthwhile.

My condition was a side effect of anesthesia, and the doctor put me on steroids. As a result, I could no longer breastfeed, and that really upset me.

Breastfeeding was an aspect of motherhood that I'd been looking forward to. It was the healthiest option for my son, and I was counting on the experience to help us bond. Lastly, I hadn't anticipated spending money on expensive infant formula.

Disappointment coupled with chronic fatigue made me very irritable. Without my niece, I would probably have fallen apart. Miriam supported me emotionally and in every other way. She cooked, cleaned, did laundry, and watched Leon so I could rest. I wondered how my mother was able to have ten babies over a fifteen-year period.

While she was with me, Miriam stayed in touch with her father and monitored his progress. Eduardo's illness was a dark cloud that loomed over us. He received experimental treatment in Mexico, and although he assured us that he felt better, we could tell he was in constant pain.

Eduardo loved to hear about Leon, but I toned down my excitement when I told him about my son. We were in different places in our lives. I finally had the baby I wanted, whereas he was going through a very difficult period.

When my mother heard of Leon's birth, she mustered the courage to call me. I did not have the heart to hang up on her. She too was worried about Eduardo, so the arrival of her latest grandchild was a welcome distraction. She asked many questions about my son and me, but she didn't dare ask any questions about the father.

Two weeks after Leon was born, Marcela came home looking rather sheepish. She took one look at him and that was it. Miriam and I barely got a chance to hold Leon while she was there.

My siblings who hurled insults at me for getting pregnant called and shamelessly asked for pictures of Leon. Not one of them was brave enough to ask who his father was or what method of conception I had settled on.

I volunteered no information because that was my business and mine alone. My child was the only person I owed an explanation, and I was prepared to give him one when he was old enough to understand.

Miriam stayed for a month, and when she left, my whole world caved in on me. Frankly, I teetered on the edge of despair. I was lonely.

A small voice constantly reminded me that people on my paternal side did not live long. It was a fear that plagued me after my father's death, and though I overcame it, Eduardo's illness brought it back. I worried about my son and wondered what would happen to him if I were not around to raise him.

Things got worse when I went back to work. I cried over the smallest issues. I had always worked mornings, and I wanted an early shift, but the only available slot was from 11 a.m. to 9:30 p.m. In my state of mind, the change in time was reason enough for a meltdown.

I found a babysitter from Peru, and I dropped Leon off on my way to work. Being away from him was much tougher than I expected. A co-worker's daughter picked him up in the afternoon and took care of him till I got there in the evening.

In hindsight, the late shift worked out best for me. I did not have to leave home at dawn, I worked only four days a week, and on most days the supervisors let me leave early.

I slowly adjusted to being a single parent and learned to cope with my feelings of sadness. Every time I felt sad or worried, I found things to do. Keeping busy quelled my anxiety.

When Leon was three months old, my only remaining uncle fell off a ladder while mending a roof. He never regained consciousness and passed away a few days later.

The death stunned our family and almost sent me into a tailspin. Though I hadn't seen my uncle often enough, it had always been a comfort to know that I had a father figure back home.

I struggled to make sense of the loss. My uncle was an accomplished helicopter pilot, larger than life, yet just like that he was gone. It was hard to understand how he'd survived so many harrowing flights only to die from an incident so humdrum.

Arabelle:

I found solace in knowing that my uncle had been able to realize his dreams and had lived passionately and fully in the time he was given. By all accounts, he'd had a good life. He had a loving family, a career he loved, and wealth.

His death gave me a new perspective on life. The man had everything he wanted yet lost what mattered most—life itself. My circumstances were not ideal; I had had to abandon my dreams, but I had a lot to be grateful for. I was alive, I had good health, and I had hope.

The loss also made see that I had placed my life on hold. Beside going to work and taking care of Leon, I did nothing. I resolved to enjoy each day. I scoured the newspapers for free and inexpensive events. I rediscovered Washington DC and immersed myself in the beautiful sights the city had to offer.

Chapter Twenty-Seven

I took Leon on his first trip to Colombia when he was five months old. Laura accompanied us, and the three of us attended Miriam's wedding in Bogota. It was a true Colombian wedding, with plenty of exquisite flowers, good food, wine, and dancing.

Miriam looked stunning when her father slowly but proudly walked her down the aisle. Eduardo had feared that he would not be around to give his only daughter away, so we were thankful to have him there.

After the wedding, Laura and I took Leon to Pereira. I was glad to see that, to a large extent, my mother still had her memory. She looked adoringly at Leon and held him for hours at a time. It was hard to believe that she was the same woman who swore she would disown me if I had a child out of wedlock. All that was in the past, and I felt closer to my mother than I'd ever been. I returned to Maryland a much happier person.

The peaceful environment was good for Laura, and she too came back happier than she'd been in years. She'd had time to reflect on her life and had concluded that practicing law was too stressful for her. She decided to go back to school and pursue a career in education. She loved history and wanted to teach the subject in high school.

Soon after our return, Laura applied to the University of Maryland and enrolled in prerequisite courses at the local community college. She was excited to be back in school and looked forward to her classes in the evenings.

The sight of Leon always brought a smile to Laura's face, and she asked if she could take care of him while I was at work. I agreed because I figured we would all benefit from the arrangement. I stayed at their home during the week, and not having to worry about Leon in the mornings certainly made my life easier.

I returned from work one afternoon to find Laura standing in the driveway. She had locked her keys in the car, with Leon still strapped in his seat. Evidently, they'd been waiting for a while. A locksmith arrived and unlocked the vehicle.

It happened again a few days later, and once more Laura had to call a locksmith. She apologized and promised to be more careful. I knew I had to make other arrangements, but I was between the proverbial rock and hard place. I was working the early-morning shift, and unless I could drop Leon off to a babysitter before 5 a.m., there was no way I could get to work on time. I prayed that there would be no more incidents.

A few weeks later, I returned to find fire trucks parked outside the Levenson home. I jumped out of my car and ran toward them. Laura had again locked the keys and my child in the vehicle. It was sweltering, and the firemen were doing all they could to get Leon out of the car. I was furious at myself for not resolving the situation sooner.

By the time the car was unlocked, Leon was drenched in sweat. A fireman checked his vital signs while a second one grilled me. When they realized that it was not the first incident, they looked at me with disdain. One of them called me aside and spoke to me sternly. I looked like a negligent mother, and I was embarrassed. I had been reluctant to give up the convenience, and in the process, I'd jeopardized Leon's life.

Considering how many kids die each summer from being accidentally locked in cars, I was fortunate. I knew I could no longer leave Leon with Laura.

I took the next day off from work so I could look for a baby-sitter. A neighbor told me about an elderly Guatemalan lady who lived on the second floor of our building. I knocked on the woman's door, told her my predicament and asked if she would watch Leon while I was at work. She agreed, on condition that I would pick him up by 4:30 p.m. each day. She cleaned offices in the city every evening and needed enough time to get to the job.

The very next morning, I took Leon downstairs on my way to work. I never again left him alone with Laura. Whenever she asked to see him, I made sure I was present.

The new babysitter's name was Dona Sofia, and she watched Leon from six in the morning till four thirty in the afternoon. I raced home each day to find her waiting outside our building with Leon. I would take her to the train station or drive her to Washington. It was tedious, but at least Leon was safe.

Dona Sofia quickly became a part of our family. When she didn't have to go to her second job, she came upstairs to my condo. We cooked and ate together, and we spent hours roaming around shopping malls.

I sensed that the woman was unhappy at home, and when I met her son, my suspicions were confirmed. I took an immediate dislike to the man. He was abrupt with his mother, and she seemed afraid of him.

Dona Sofia told me that her son had moved in with her when he fell on hard times. He never moved out, he refused to work, paid no bills, and constantly demanded money from her. She endured the treatment because she had no one to turn to. Her other children were back in Guatemala, and her son had driven away the few friends she had. She did have a cousin in Southern Maryland, but she was too embarrassed to tell him about her problem.

Marcela and I kept Dona Sofia close to us, and whenever the son snapped at her in our presence, we rebuked him. On one occasion when he was belligerent toward us, I informed him that if I ever suspected that he'd physically abused his mother, I would call the police. He seemed shocked and backed off quickly.

His mother confirmed what I thought might have been the reason for his hasty retreat. He was in the country illegally. There was also a warrant for his arrest for driving while intoxicated.

After my encounter with her son, Dona Sofia took care of Leon in my home. I didn't want the man anywhere near my child. The new arrangement was convenient for me, and things went well for a while.

When Leon was about eighteen months old, I noticed changes in Dona Sofia that alarmed me. She was often absent-minded and uncharacteristically irritable. She also talked to herself constantly. I recognized those signs; I had seen the same symptoms in my mother. I knew I had to find Dona Sofia help and find Leon another babysitter.

Luckily for me, Rosalinda moved to Maryland from Alabama about the same time, so she watched Leon while I was at work. Dona Sofia continued to spend time with us, and I kept an eye on her. She turned down all my offers to take her to a doctor. She didn't have health insurance, and she was not willing to go through the State to get healthcare.

I tried to talk to her son, and he made it amply clear that he was not interested in anything I had to say. Since I was not a family member, there wasn't much else I could do.

Rosalinda was great with Leon, but I was concerned about her too. Her daughter had told me that she was unhappy—I could not have imagined the extent of her sadness. She was wistful, and the only time she smiled was when she interacted with Leon. She said very little, and any attempt on my part to start a conversation seemed like an intrusion on her thoughts. I did all I could to cheer Rosalinda up and planned different activities when Marcela was home on weekends. Rosalinda usually tuned us out and retreated to her favorite corner. She was not the person I used to know.

Even as a young girl, Rosalinda had been very dynamic. She was self-motivated, and nothing could keep her down. The woman who showed up at my home was withdrawn and had some of the same characteristics as Laura.

I tried to get Rosalinda professional counseling, but she turned it down. On the rare occasions when she chose to talk, it was invariably about the job she had lost. She was still nursing the wounds from being forced out of her position with the Colombian government.

Rosalinda had risen through the ranks and had expected to remain with the agency till she retired. Leaving prematurely and without a retirement package almost destroyed her. When she moved to Alabama, she thought she would find new opportunities. Like Marcela, she spoke hardly any English and was limited in what she could do. That was when she gave up on life.

I empathized with Rosalinda because I know what it feels like to be derailed from one's aspirations. I was also objective about her situation. What happened to her was a common practice in Colombia. Just as my godfather made concessions for my father and for her, someone else probably needed to make room for their relative. They subsequently got rid of her and reassigned the position without a care as to how it affected her.

Rosalinda could not let go or move on. She wallowed in self-pity and let bitterness get the better of her. I frequently pointed out people who were doctors, engineers, lawyers, and accountants in their countries yet worked as cab drivers, parking lot attendants, couriers, and babysitters in the United States. None of that made a difference to her, and even though I tried to be patient, I sometimes lost my temper. I could not believe that I had another depressed person on my hands.

Having both of my sisters with me was nothing like I had hoped for. They left me weary and frustrated. They constantly complained about the system and the lack of opportunities for Latinos. My sisters failed to understand that to be successful in any country, you have to speak the language.

My contention was that unless they possessed unique or sought-after-skills, non-Spanish-speaking people could not expect to be wildly successful in Latin America. Similarly, Latinos who possessed no special skills yet refused to speak English could not expect to find great opportunities in mainstream America. We debated that topic till I got sick of it.

There were days when I wanted to take Leon and run far away from my sisters. With a demanding job, a baby, an ailing mother, and bills to pay, I didn't need any more stress.

Chapter Twenty-Eight

*I*n January of 2007, Laura showed remarkable improvement. She had been in and out of rehabilitation programs in Dallas, Boston, and Baltimore, and she'd finally found one that helped her. She became more active and took more interest in her family. She was back in college after taking a few semesters off, and although we were cautiously optimistic, we believed that she was on her way to recovery.

We were thankful for Laura's progress. It had been over a decade since her problems began. She'd had many episodes of drug overdose and had caused us plenty of anxiety. She almost died from a cocktail of pills and alcohol while visiting her older daughter at school in Michigan.

Again and again, Josh and the two older kids had gone home to find Laura unconscious. Because of that, Josh always made sure that someone else was home when Melissa got back from school. He'd called me on many occasions when the older kids weren't home and he couldn't leave the office. "Please hurry and get to the house before Melissa gets home," he would plead. Fortunately, I was usually home from work by then, and I would drop whatever I was doing and race to get there. I would run errands with Melissa, or we would stay at the house and wait for her father or her siblings to return.

In addition to the accidental overdoses, Laura had made conscious attempts to end her life. On one occasion, she'd tried to jump off a bridge, and the police had had to talk her out of it.

She seemed to have all that behind her, and we were ready for a new beginning. I spent most of my Saturdays with them, and it was almost like old times. The mood in the house was much lighter and everyone was smiling more.

On a Tuesday in March, I was on a lunch break and decided to treat myself to a nice lunch. I had just paid for my sandwich when my phone rang. It was Josh. "She did it this time, and it was Melissa who found her," he said quietly. He didn't need to say anything else; I knew exactly what he meant.

I dropped my food and ran. I was hysterical. I got permission to leave work and went straight to their home. The drive, which normally took half an hour, took fifteen minutes that day.

The medical examiner had removed Laura's body, but there were cops all over the home. A detective was aggressively questioning Melissa. He seemed irritated that she could not remember the exact time when she found her mother, or the position she was lying in. The poor child was shaking and unable to speak coherently. I was so angry; I grabbed Melissa and yelled at the detective to stop.

Surprised by the outburst, the man demanded to know who I was. I ignored him and tried to take Melissa inside the house. He did not appreciate the interruption, and the two of us got into a screaming match.

Josh calmed both of us down. Melissa and I went inside, where we found her sister totally distraught. I could not console the girls. They were in shock and unable to tell me what had happened.

After several hours, the cops finally left, and Josh told me the details. He had called home to see if he'd dropped his fountain pen on the way out. Melissa was home on spring break and answered the phone. When she went into her parents' bedroom to look for the pen, she found her mother on the floor of the closet. She ran to tell her father that her mother had fallen down.

"Get Karen!" he recalled yelling into the phone. Melissa went downstairs to get her sister while her father called for an ambulance. Karen was a volunteer paramedic with a fire station nearby, and she knew how to administer CPR. In spite of the efforts to resuscitate her mother, she remained unresponsive. Karen kept trying till the responding unit arrived and pronounced Laura dead.

It was a dark day for us; our worst fears had come to pass. Josh always worried that Melissa would one day find her mother dead, and that was exactly what happened. Word travelled quickly through the neighborhood, and people arrived at the house to console Josh and the children.

The timing of the death shocked those who knew Laura. It came at a time when she appeared to be doing very well. She had been communicating a lot more with friends and neighbors, and she was certainly enjoying her studies. She had just purchased a ticket to visit my mother in Colombia and intended to spend the whole summer there.

I firmly believe that Laura was not trying to take her life on that fateful day. She had told me just a few days earlier that she had not been sleeping well. She was "looking for that deep sleep," she'd said.

I am certain that the quest for sound sleep made Laura take the sleeping pills which ultimately killed her. After sixteen failed attempts at suicide, Laura was gone. Gone at a time when she wasn't trying to kill herself.

Her parents arrived on the day she passed away. Her mother's tone was accusatory, and she blamed her daughter's problems and subsequent death on the pressures of her job. She also said her son-in-law ought to have done more to save her daughter. If she'd visited more often, she would have known that Josh did everything he could to save Laura.

The poor man was reeling from his wife's death. His twenty-two year old son took charge and made the funeral arrangements. Adam worked with precision and conferred with their rabbi to make sure he observed all Jewish customs.

I personally believe that for years, Adam had been preparing himself mentally. He knew that it was just a matter of time before prescription drugs claimed his mother's life.

Following Jewish tradition, the funeral should have been held within twenty-four hours of Laura's death. Due to the circumstances, an autopsy had to be conducted before the body could be released to the funeral home.

The family donated Laura's brain to science, and even though I knew it would help in medical research, it bothered me immensely. To me, she had been robbed yet again. Robbed of life and then of what made her unique: her powerful brain.

The funeral was well-planned, and the synagogue was filled to capacity. Only family members were supposed to go into the room where the body was, but I was allowed to go in because Melissa wanted me to take her.

Laura looked like she'd finally found the peace that had eluded her for so long. Looking at her, I remembered the words she'd spoken just a few days earlier. "I need that deep sleep."

"What a waste, what a waste!" I said over and over again as Melissa and I held each other. How could someone with so much promise end up in a casket in the prime of her life? She was only 47 years old. Like my late uncle, Laura had the opportunity to pursue her dreams. Like him, she had achieved her goals, but her career and life were tragically cut short.

Watching Laura lowered into a grave that afternoon, was by far one of the most painful experiences of my life. When we returned to the house, it seemed empty. Although the Laura we knew had departed years earlier, we still felt a void. She was gone for good, and so was the hope we'd held on to for so long. There was no chance of her overcoming depression and addiction. Those cruel and unrelenting illnesses had taken her from us.

I moved about the house like a robot, staring at pictures of Laura. I pressed her sweater to my chest as I folded her clothes. It hurt so much. The lady had taken me in, treated me like family, and taught me to believe in myself. I know that had she not been ill, she would have pushed me to greater heights.

Following Jewish tradition, I covered all the mirrors in the house to mark the beginning of *Shiva.* During the week-long period of mourning, the family constantly received guests. I felt sorry for them because I knew they would have liked to be alone for a while.

The children began their eleven-month obligation to recite special prayers for their mother. I still get emotional when I remember how they sobbed while praying.

For the next few weeks, I spent time with the family, and I felt a strange sense of calm when I was there. I could tell Laura was happy and free.

Shortly after her death, Leon was playing with a train set she'd given him. Although he was by himself, he seemed to be carrying on a conversation with someone.

"Who are you talking to?" I asked him.

"Auntie Laura!" he replied, pointing at a spot beside him. He seemed surprised that I asked the question.

I know we have an angel watching over us.

Chapter Twenty-Nine

Laura had always wanted Melissa to earn a high school diploma and not a certificate. I felt obligated to see to it that Melissa fulfilled her mother's wishes.

During her final year of high school, Melissa wanted to live with me, and her father allowed her to do so. That enabled me to monitor her closely. I helped her with her Spanish assignments, and twice a week a tutor helped her with the other subjects.

I am still not sure who cried more when Melissa did her homework. She cried from frustration while I cried from despair. The poor child was grieving and ready to give up on school. I had many heated one-way conversations with her mother and berated the dead woman for leaving me in a situation that I was ill-equipped to handle.

There were days when Melissa really missed her mother, and it was heartbreaking to watch her grieve. I would withdraw to the bathroom and have a quiet conversation with Laura. I asked her to pray for me so I would have the strength and wisdom to help the family she loved and left behind.

Josh and Karen also struggled emotionally, and there were days when they fell apart. Though Adam did not show it outwardly, I knew he too was in pain. I did all I could to support the family. I couldn't ease their sorrow, so I prayed a lot and asked God to console them.

We somehow persevered, and in May of 2009, Melissa graduated from high school. The whole family was there, and we cheered loudly. Tears cascaded down my cheeks, and I noticed that other family members were crying too. We were all thinking of the odds that Melissa had had to overcome in order to earn the diploma. We were also keenly aware of the one person who was missing.

After the graduation ceremony, we went out to celebrate. For the first time in a long while, the family had something to rejoice about. Melissa basked in the attention, and she wanted her special moment to last forever.

After dinner, Marcela, Leon, Melissa, her dog, and I piled into my old minivan and sang songs all the way back to Silver Spring. I couldn't have been more proud of Melissa. That night, I thanked God for answering my prayers.

Melissa, Leon, and I left for Colombia a few days later. We spent a week in Pereira, and then we went to Bogota to visit Eduardo and his daughter. Miriam was expecting and looked radiant. Leon and Melissa were excited at the prospect of having a new baby in the family, and I promised to take them back to Bogota as soon as the baby arrived.

Chapter Thirty

$\mathcal{S}$hortly after our return to Maryland, Miriam was rushed to the hospital with complications to her pregnancy. The doctors discovered a large mass in her uterus. As time went by, the mass outgrew the baby, and there was concern that it would suffocate the child. It also put Miriam's life at risk.

Eduardo was so worried about his daughter, his own health declined. As the weeks went by, we became more anxious about Miriam, her baby and her father.

The baby girl finally arrived in August, and though she was healthy, Miriam remained weak. She was confined to her bed and had to wait eight months before the mass could be removed.

We thought that after surgery Miriam would return to normal, but instead we almost lost her. She hemorrhaged internally and went into a coma. There were many hairy moments, and we feared that if anything happened to her, it would have a ripple effect. Eduardo would lose the will to live, and if anything happened to him, our mother would die from grief.

I called each day to check on Miriam and her father. Eduardo was scared, and he sometimes sobbed so much he could barely get his words out. Just when I was truly beginning to despair, Miriam came out of the coma.

I was able to get time off from work, and I took Leon to Colombia to see Miriam and the baby. We also visited Eduardo, and I was surprised at his emotional state.

My brother's temperament had changed. He was angry all the time, and he was especially short-fused with Leon. He snapped at my son constantly, and that confused the child because they'd always had a great relationship.

I knew Eduardo was having a hard time coming to terms with his condition, so I bit my tongue. Like everyone else, he wanted to live and accomplish his goals. Unfortunately, he was battling a disease that could end his life.

The atmosphere was so tense, I decided to leave Bogota and go to Pereira. I needed to put distance between us, so I wouldn't say things I would later regret.

Eduardo insisted on going to Pereira with us, and that was awkward. Somehow, he completely missed the cue that I was leaving because of him. His daughter told him that he wasn't well enough to travel, but he would not be dissuaded.

My mother wept when she saw Eduardo. The long trip weakened him, and he was even more irritable. As much as I kept Leon out of sight, Eduardo found fault with my son. The tension mounted, and I finally exploded. Some harsh words were spoken, and for the rest of the trip I said nothing to him.

Before I left Pereira, Alejandro called to announce that after thirty years in Canada, he was returning home. He'd retired from his teaching job at the university in Montreal, and he and his first wife were planning to build and operate a resort in Colombia.

The concept was to get away from the conventional and build rustic log cabins where people could be one with nature. The resort would serve as a retreat for companies, churches, married couples, and groups seeking serenity.

They'd chosen the eastern coast of the country and decided on a location in the lush mountains of Parque Tayrona, which overlooked the Caribbean Sea.

I thought it was an intriguing idea, though with his bohemian lifestyle, I was unsure how Alejandro would fare as a businessman in Colombia. I also questioned his choice of a business partner. His ex-wife Evelyn was wild, and that concerned me. A Caucasian woman in a small Colombian town draws attention. A wild white woman fraternizing with unsavory locals could draw attention from the wrong people.

I framed my concerns delicately because Alejandro had the strangest relationship with his ex-wives. They were his closest friends, and he did not entertain disparaging comments about them. He brushed aside my apprehensions and told me that he'd made up his mind.

My siblings tried to discourage Alejandro from returning to Colombia and especially from taking Evelyn with him. It was pointless; they had already sold their homes and shipped their belongings.

Alejandro and Evelyn went ahead with their plans, and within a few months they were back in Colombia. Leon and I visited them in the fall of 2009, and that was one of the best vacations I had ever taken.

They lived in the small fishing village of Taganga, in a beautiful house perched on a cliff, just yards from the Caribbean Sea. A vine-covered terrace wrapped around the home, and hundreds of clusters of grapes hung just inches above our heads.

They had a garden full of exotic plants, and equally exotic birds circled feeders in the trees. The fragrance of jasmine bushes filled the air.

The home had bright spacious rooms with paintings, freshly cut flowers, and potted plants everywhere. The sea breeze constantly strummed wind chimes and tossed white lace curtains in and out of large French windows. I felt like the minute we arrived, the breeze blew all my problems away.

Alejandro had three big beautiful dogs that ran freely through the house. Leon fell in love with the animals and constantly chased after them. Alejandro taught him to swim and draw, and he let him walk the dogs on the beach and through the neighborhood. Several neighbors stopped by to chat, and it seemed like Alejandro and Evelyn were well-liked in their community.

My brother took us up to the mountains and showed us the site where construction had already begun. He was passionate about the project, and it was easy to see why. The location was alluring. It was peaceful, the air was clean, and the scenery was spectacular. It was the perfect place to go to retreat from the world.

The days flew by quickly, and when it was time to return to Maryland, Leon clung to Alejandro and refused to leave Taganga. I promised him that we'd visit his uncle every year. I had every intention of keeping that promise; I was eager to return when the resort was completed.

I assured the rest of the family that Alejandro's idea was a great one. Everyone was excited, and we all planned to be there for the grand opening. Even Marcela planned to be there. Her intention was to go back home and work for Alejandro. She was going to "kiss America goodbye, get on a plane to Colombia, and become somebody."

Rosalinda came alive whenever we discussed the project; she too had plans. She talked about managing the resort for Alejandro. I chuckled each time she brought up the subject because I knew Alejandro was in for a challenge. I joked that once my sisters arrived, he would need to go somewhere else to find tranquility.

Alejandro sent pictures of the construction almost every week, and we were surprised at how fast the builders were working. He and Evelyn had the funds to purchase materials and pay for labor, so there were no delays. They were far ahead of schedule.

Chapter Thirty-One

*I*n February of 2010, I received a very disturbing call from Alberto. It was the beginning of what was to become a turbulent year for my family. Alberto was scrambling to raise $10,000 for Alejandro.

The buildings in Parque Tayrona had attracted the attention of a local cartel, and the thugs were demanding money. They made it clear that unless they received payment, Alejandro would not be allowed to complete his construction.

Such a statement from a cartel could mean anything. They could take over the buildings, burn them down—worse still, they could kill my brother. I didn't have $10,000, and I didn't believe that paying the cartel would solve the problem. I told Alberto as much. My argument was that if the thugs were demanding money even before the project was complete, they would definitely return when the resort was opened.

I was afraid for Alejandro because when the cartels set their sights on a person, they do not stop till the victim is dead or totally ruined. Even after their demands are met, they sometimes kill their victims to affirm their reputation of ruthlessness.

I called Alejandro and begged him to drop everything and return to Montreal. "Your life is worth more than the buildings," I pleaded with him. His ex-wife would not abandon the project, and he was not prepared to leave her in Colombia all by herself. He was confident that making the payment would keep the thugs off his back for a while but anticipated that they would demand monthly payments when the project was complete.

I was furious with Alejandro, and I could not believe that he and Evelyn could be so reckless. Despite my many attempts to reach her and talk some sense into her, Evelyn would not speak to me. I knew that unless she left Colombia, Alejandro would remain there, even at the risk of losing his life.

Alberto called a few more times that month and urged me to find the money. He even suggested that I borrow against my condominium. I knew I wouldn't qualify for a loan, and even if I did, I couldn't afford the monthly payments. I was adamant that the only solution was for Alejandro to leave Colombia. My brothers were upset with me, and for the better part of the year, I heard nothing from either one of them.

The frantic telephone calls resumed toward the end of October. Evelyn notified Alejandro's other ex-wife and his daughters that she'd neither seen nor heard from him in almost two weeks.

She had allegedly returned to the house on October 17th to find Alejandro gone. She waited two days before filing a missing persons report. The police purportedly dismissed her because they thought Alejandro might have left home after a fight.

Alejandro had always been a free spirit and was known to take off unceremoniously. Years prior, he'd disappeared for eight months. He later surfaced barefoot in Pereira after hitch-hiking all the way from British Columbia, Canada. This time however, we knew he hadn't left voluntarily. I prayed that his captors would not torture or kill him.

I called Evelyn and fired questions at her. I could not get a straight story out of the woman. I wanted to know when she last saw Alejandro and where. I wanted to know where she'd been since his disappearance. Above all, I wanted to know exactly how much she knew about the demand for money. Her answers frustrated me, and I eventually hung up on her.

I was unable to go to Colombia, but I prompted one of my nephews to contact the authorities in Taganga. The police were reluctant to get involved, and after waiting several days for them to start an investigation, I went to the Canadian Embassy in Washington.

Since Alejandro was a naturalized Canadian citizen, the consulate immediately called their embassy in Bogota. The Canadian officials in Bogota contacted the head of police in Colombia. Only then did the Taganga police start investigating my brother's disappearance. By then, Evelyn was nowhere to be found.

My nephew accompanied a SWAT team to Alejandro's home to see if they could find any clues. Although we expected the worst, we were not prepared for the videos he sent as things unfolded.

There were "for sale" signs posted on the wall surrounding the house. The gate was unlocked, and when the team went in, they found the dogs on the terrace, chained to a post. It was evident that the animals had not been fed in weeks. They were unable to stand, and they looked nothing like the big beautiful dogs I saw when I visited.

Alejandro and Evelyn were gone, and the house had been emptied of all furniture and everything else. Doors and windows were gone. Naked electrical wires dangled from ceilings and sockets. Appliances, sinks, shelves, cabinets, curtain rods—every fixture was gone. Even the bathtubs and commodes had been removed. There wasn't a single item of clothing or a piece of paper in sight.

The police were not surprised; they had seen similar cases. They explained that it was a common practice for the cartels to abduct a homeowner, extort money from the family, kill the victim, and take over the home. They rent or sell the property to someone else and repeat the process. Colombians living outside the country and looking to return home were the usual prey.

When the SWAT team left the house, they sent my nephew back to Bogota and asked him not to return to Taganga. They suspected that more than likely, someone in the neighborhood was involved and was watching the house. Returning alone could lead to yet another kidnapping.

The local police located Evelyn. She was still in Taganga and still cavorting with the locals. Officials from the Canadian embassy convinced her to leave the country and stay away until the case was solved.

I continued to press her for answers, but nothing she said made sense to me. I couldn't establish where she was when the house was emptied, and she couldn't tell me why she abandoned their dogs. There was no doubt in my mind that she knew a lot more than she admitted to.

With the Canadian embassy breathing down their necks, the Colombian authorities worked hard, but to no avail. They repeatedly called the number on the "for sale" signs posted on the wall. The calls went unanswered, and the line was eventually disconnected.

The neighbors didn't know anything, or so they said. I know someone had to have seen trucks moving things out of the house. I wondered if any of the neighbors I met could have been part of the conspiracy.

I wanted to believe that Alejandro was alive. His daughters on the other hand were convinced that their father had been killed. The younger of the two wanted to go to Taganga because she believed that she would find her father's remains. The family put a stop to her plans; we didn't need any more casualties.

It was a troubling time, and the ordeal greatly affected Eduardo. He was distraught, and within months, the cancer returned and attacked his other kidney. Alberto and I both flew home to see him.

I took the opportunity to question them about the circumstances surrounding Alejandro's disappearance. Alberto was evasive, and Eduardo staved off any discussion on the topic. It was clear that there was a lot they were not saying.

I sensed tension between them and our brother Rafael. They had a private meeting with him, and while I could not hear them, the gestures were telling. Rafael hung his head, and after a while he got up and left. Eduardo and Alberto hurled insults after him, yet he did not say a word.

I had never known Rafael to run away from a fight, so I knew he'd done something terribly wrong. I was convinced that he was somehow involved in Alejandro's disappearance.

For the next couple of days, I followed Alberto and Eduardo around the house, imploring them to tell me what they were hiding. Eduardo would not entertain any questions, and he didn't want to hear Rafael's name. When I persisted, he yelled at me and hobbled away.

Alberto finally admitted that he'd sent Rafael money to pay off the kidnappers. He didn't know how much of the money Rafael delivered or what happened to the rest of it. He did know that the cartel threatened to kill Alejandro because they didn't receive the full amount. They demanded the outstanding balance with interest, but he couldn't raise any more money.

I wanted to know how the cartel communicated, whom they spoke to, and where the money was delivered. Alberto wouldn't answer those questions, and instead he asked me to drop the matter.

I went to the police to check on their progress and to give them the additional information I had. Eduardo and Alberto were absolutely incensed! They thought I was jeopardizing my life and theirs because the cartel could have had informants within the police department.

For months, we did not tell our mother about Alejandro's disappearance. We didn't tell her about Eduardo's worsening condition either. Oddly enough, she called out their names repeatedly, and they were the only people she asked for in her moments of clarity.

Eduardo eventually told her what we had been hiding from her. She cried so hard we thought she would literally die. Thankfully, she slipped back into her world and forgot everything Eduardo had told her. The very next morning, she picked up the telephone and tried to call Alejandro. She also asked repeatedly for her two daughters.

Marcela, Rosalinda, and I called her, but she did not acknowledge us. Instead, she made frenzied demands to see her daughters Ines and Gloria. We chalked it up to her dementia. She had lost an infant daughter long before I was born, and her name was Carolina. We didn't have relatives, friends or neighbors named Ines and Gloria, and we had no idea why she picked those names.

She was unrelenting in her demands to see her "imaginary daughters," so Alberto humored her and promised to find them. That quieted her to some degree, but she still asked about them daily.

Chapter Thirty-Two

s if we weren't dealing with a lot already, my mother fell in the bathtub, fractured her hip, and had to be hospitalized. A doctor took her off the medication she had been taking for two years, and the results were astounding. All the symptoms of dementia disappeared, and she had complete clarity.

We thought it was a temporary condition, yet day after day she communicated with a sound mind. Alberto teased her about the "mystery daughters" she had been asking for, and what happened next could very well have been from a movie.

My mother calmly divulged that she had been molested by a much older man when she was just a child. It allegedly went on for years, and she consequently became pregnant at the age of fourteen. The man was a powerful figure in their town, and her parents did not have the resources to go up against him. Back then, the police didn't necessarily help victims; they worked in favor of those who could pay them.

To cover up the scandal, the man took her in, and she eventually had two children by him. Their names were Ines and Gloria Rivera. She claimed that the man and his sisters treated her like a slave and beat her constantly. She was not allowed to leave the house, and she was often locked up in a room with no food. Fearing that they would eventually kill her, her mother advised her to get out at the first opportunity and leave the children behind.

According to my mother, the man made the mistake of leaving the gate unlocked when he went out one morning. She grabbed a few clothes and a couple of pictures, climbed through the window, and ran away. She never went back and never contacted the man. He did not bother to find her, and he never notified her parents of her disappearance.

After her escape, her mother sent her to a convent in Pasto to become a nun. That did not work out because she missed her children and could not focus on her studies. Soon after she left the convent, she met and married my father.

I thought the story was absurd. I could not picture my mother climbing through a window or running away from a man. She stuck to her story and gave us the dates of birth of her alleged daughters, begging us to find them.

Still convinced that my mother was hallucinating, I asked her questions about unrelated incidents to see if she could correctly remember facts. She answered all my questions accurately.

I asked her about the infant daughter she lost, and she told me the child's name, the age at which she passed away, and the circumstances surrounding her death. She went on to remind me about a strange incident we witnessed when we visited the cemetery where the child was buried.

It was the only time we ever visited the child's grave, and while we were there, a family arrived to bury their loved one. Two of the pallbearers immediately caught our attention. They were elderly, and they stumbled as they brought up the rear.

Colombian cemeteries usually have layers of vaults that rise several stories above the ground. The vault to which the procession was headed, was about ten feet high. The men had to climb onto a scaffold, lift the casket above their heads, and slide it into the chamber.

The two elderly men buckled under the weight. They angled the casket so much it was diagonal. The rest of the pallbearers struggled to level off their load. The casket swayed dangerously. The lid popped open; the corpse sailed out and landed face down with a loud thud.

The pallbearers in question let go of the coffin and bolted. In their flight, they knocked mourners to the ground. In a country where people are superstitious about the dead, it was an abomination.

Our first instinct was to run. We ran after the pallbearers, with some of the mourners on our heels. We did not stop till we were out of the cemetery and on the other side of the road. By then, I'd lost the heel of one shoe and the sole of the other.

We caught up with one of the elderly pallbearers. The man reeked of alcohol, and he was panting so hard we thought he would keel over. When we asked him if he was alright, he glared at us and muttered a string of expletives. In his opinion, the corpse was uncooperative. He hailed a passing truck, climbed in the back, and left.

It was the first and only time I saw my mother unrestrained. She laughed till tears ran down her face, and for years, she talked about that incident.

I was amazed that my mother recalled every detail of the trip to the cemetery, but I still didn't believe that she had two other daughters. She was adamant about it, so I jokingly suggested that we look for her "mystery daughters" on Facebook.

I logged in and practically fell out of my chair! There were two sisters in South Brunswick, New Jersey, with matching names, and they were from my mother's hometown of Cali. Not only did the women exist, the older one was a spitting image of my mother.

Countless questions raced through my mind. Was there credibility to her story? Did she ever tell my father about those daughters, or did she hide it from him too? What other secrets could she be harboring? As prim and proper as my mom always was, it was hard to believe that she had such a dark and troubled past.

Shock rippled through the family, and we demanded more information. My mother produced a picture of a man and two little girls. I remembered seeing pictures of that same man when I was much younger. She had told us that he was a relative, and I remembered her saying that he'd died in an accident. None of us had ever seen pictures of the girls.

The revelation explained a lot about my mother. She always had a melancholy air about her, and there was always an invisible barrier that prevented my sisters and me from getting too close. She probably felt guilty about taking care of us when she'd abandoned her first two daughters.

We had several conference calls to determine how best to approach the ladies. I found a picture of my mother when she was their age and posted it on their Facebook pages. My hope was that out of curiosity they would contact me.

Weeks went by, and I heard nothing from the women. Slowly, the enthusiasm waned, and we concluded that they did not want to be bothered.

In April of 2011, the younger of the two sisters contacted Juan Carlos's wife via Facebook. Gloria asked several questions about the family, and she asked my sister-in-law to coordinate a meeting with my mother.

While the rest of us were excited, Eduardo did all he could to deter our mother from meeting with the woman. He claimed that he didn't want our mother's image to be tarnished. The explanation seemed odd to me, and I wondered if once again Eduardo knew more than he was saying.

I happened to be in Pereira when Gloria and a friend arrived from Cali. We shook hands and spoke briefly. There were no hugs or tears; it was like meeting any other stranger for the first time.

It was, however, surreal to see the woman with my mother. The daughters we thought were figments of her imagination were real, and one of them was sitting in her living room. They talked about the trip from Cali, the weather, and everything else. Nobody broached the all-important topic.

I ordered Chinese food and served our guests. After the meal, Gloria finally brought up the subject of her visit. I felt uncomfortable, and since I was returning to Maryland that day, I excused myself so I could get ready.

I still heard everything that was said. Gloria asked many questions. Her tone was not accusatory; she simply wanted to know why my mother left them and never returned. As difficult as it was for her, my mother told Gloria in a steady voice the same story she'd told us.

I listened for Gloria's reaction, but there was only a long awkward silence. The woman must have believed some of what she heard, because she did not jump up and defend her father like I would have done.

I didn't envy Gloria's position. She'd grown up believing that her mother died when she was an infant. When her mother surfaced, it was to tell her that her father, the only parent she'd known, was a monster.

According to Gloria, her father was still alive and living in Cali. I tried to visualize the conversation that would ensue between father and daughter when she returned home.

Despite the bombshell my mother dropped on them, Gloria and her friend spent the rest of the afternoon with her, went to their hotel for the night, and returned to see her again the next day.

Chapter Thirty-Three

arcela and Rosalinda asked a million questions when I got home, and they were disappointed that I didn't have enough answers. They were ready to get on the highway to New Jersey to bond with their newly discovered sisters. I chose to wait for an invitation. I thought it was best to give the ladies time to deal with the shocking revelation before descending on them.

Months went by, and we heard nothing from our estranged sisters. My mother constantly asked for them, and with time her hopes of a lasting reunion turned into anguish. I tried numerous times to reach the women, and they ignored me. They finally blocked us from contacting them via Facebook.

I have no doubt that their father had a totally different version of what happened. If he was capable of sexually abusing a child, then honesty was probably not one of his strengths.

Nonetheless, just as I was inclined to believe my mother, the women may have chosen to believe their father over a stranger. Even if they believed the story, they probably resented her for abandoning them. I can't blame them; my mother should have contacted them decades earlier.

The symptoms of dementia returned. My mom was agitated and rambled about events of her childhood. It was evident that she'd felt tormented for most of her life. She yearned for her two oldest children and constantly asked us to find them.

Different feelings were unearthed when we discovered our sisters. After the initial shock, we were anxious to get to know them. We already had a large family, but there was plenty of room for two more siblings. We were disappointed when they blocked us on Facebook, but we had to respect the fact that they wanted nothing to do with us.

Eduardo was upset with me for finding the women. In his opinion, I'd caused our mother unnecessary pain. We argued constantly, and things got pretty tense between us. I didn't back down because I was convinced that my mother had a right to look for the children she was forced to abandon.

About the same time, I was embroiled in a feud with Diego. Alberto and I kept hiring caregivers for our mother, and none of them lasted. They would stay for a week or two and leave. It turned out that Diego made it impossible for anyone to stick around. He spent the money we sent for our mother's upkeep, and thanks to him, her prescriptions were not filled regularly.

When I heard that, I called Diego and rained curses on his head. By the time I hung up the phone, I was hoarse and my blood pressure was elevated. Every time I called my mother, he would intercept the call and we would have another screaming match.

Just when I thought my siblings could not frustrate me any further, Eduardo remarried his ex-wife. I was dumbfounded. I couldn't believe that he would do something so stupid. Since we were not speaking to each other, I couldn't tell him what I thought of his lack of judgment.

There was a lot more chaos in the family, and Rosalinda went to Colombia to resolve some of the issues. Her green card had just arrived, five long years after she started the process.

Shortly after Rosalinda arrived in Pereira, our mother suffered yet another heart attack. Rosalinda took her back and forth to Bogota, where stents were placed in her heart.

Trying to rectify the problems at home proved stressful for Rosalinda, and within a couple of weeks, she too suffered a heart attack. Fortunately for her, Alberto was in Colombia at the time, and he made sure that she received the necessary care.

I was shaken to think we could have lost Rosalinda, and that prompted me to call a truce with Eduardo. He was glad that I called, and before long we were speaking regularly.

I went to Colombia to visit him, and as we customarily did, we took a long road trip together. We drove to Cali for a couple of days, and I took the opportunity to ask him why he had remarried his ex-wife. He covered his face with both hands and shook his head. He said he was sick and lonely and thought it would be a second chance at happiness. When I asked how things were going, he was quiet for a long time before admitting that he'd made a mistake.

He seemed vulnerable, and I thought I could capitalize on his weakness. I brought up the issue of Alejandro's disappearance, hoping to get long-awaited answers out of him. He gave me a stern look and told me to let it go.

On our way back to Bogota, Eduardo stopped in the small town of Ginebra Valle, which was famous for its cuisine. He said he'd been craving their signature soup for months.

While we were looking for a restaurant, a motorcyclist ploughed into us and wrecked the back of Eduardo's car. We were fortunate to escape with very minor injuries.

Eduardo was shaken and wanted to get back on the road immediately, but I insisted on finding the restaurant. There were too many days when he was left to fend for himself, so I wanted him to have the food he'd been craving.

The soup was called sancocho, and it was made of chicken and vegetables. It was delicious, and Eduardo talked about returning to the restaurant at a later date. I wondered silently if he would ever travel that way again.

Back in the car, we were both quiet. I had a feeling the trip to Cali would be our last. Though I tried to hide my tears, Eduardo noticed. He took my hand and thanked me for accompanying him. I looked up and saw that he too had been crying. I was glad that we had set aside our differences.

Chapter Thirty-Four

I returned home and went about my life quietly. I called my mother and Eduardo every week, and I could tell that they were both declining. More often than not, my mother was incoherent. She cried even more and continued to ask for Gloria and Ines. It was depressing to call her, but I had a duty to do so.

Eduardo was struggling physically and emotionally. He was getting weaker by the day, and he was constantly in pain. The pain kept him up at night, and since that supposedly disturbed his wife, she moved him out of their bedroom and onto a mattress in the den. He feared that if something happened to him in the middle of the night, she wouldn't know.

The woman was a physician, so I didn't understand how she could be so callous toward him. Even though they lived together, Eduardo had to go to his daughter's house for his meals. I know he was always happy to see his daughter and grandchild, but for a sick person, it was a hardship to make the trip daily.

By the fall of that year, my brother was really suffering, and I wanted to see him. I repeatedly asked for time off from work, and all my requests were ignored. Miriam called me at the end of November to let me know that her father had taken a turn for the worse.

I immediately called my job. It was a Sunday night, so of course there was no one in the office. I left the station manager a message that I had to leave for Colombia. I didn't care if it cost me my job; I had to see my brother one last time.

I was also hoping that, knowing his life was ending, Eduardo would tell me what he knew about Alejandro's disappearance. I prayed that he would be alive and alert when I got there.

The quickest way to get to Bogota was via Avianca's direct flight from Dulles Airport. There was only one flight scheduled for the following day, and it was full. Eduardo's wife pulled some strings, and even though I was not qualified to do so, I sat in a jump seat all the way to Bogota.

I went straight to the hospital, and, mercifully, Eduardo was still clinging to life and actually greeted me with a grin. He'd aged tremendously and had lost even more weight than I expected. He hugged me tightly and assured me that he was okay. I fought back tears.

When he tried to sit up, the blanket fell off his legs. I gasped. His legs were huge! He tried to make light of it, but I could no longer hold my tears. I stepped out of the room and let go of the emotions I had been suppressing.

I spoke to Eduardo's doctor, who explained that because his kidney and liver were not functioning properly, his body was retaining fluids—hence the swollen legs.

I asked the question no one ever wants to ask a doctor about a loved one. He gave me the answer I was dreading: Eduardo had only a few days to live. Their focus was no longer on curing him or slowing down the cancer. They were merely managing his pain and keeping him as comfortable as possible.

For the next few days, I stayed by my brother's side, leaving only when his wife and daughter arrived in the evenings. We reminisced about good times, and he told me about things he wanted to do. He sounded like someone who expected to make a full recovery. He did not talk about his impending death, and even though I wanted to ask what his final wishes were, I could not bring up the topic.

I reported his condition to my other siblings daily, and I had a hard time convincing them that he was dying. He was upbeat when he spoke to them, so they thought I was being unduly pessimistic.

Six days after I got there, Eduardo had a very rough time. I was certain that we were losing him. That was when he mentioned that the end was near. He said he knew his organs were shutting down because he was experiencing sensations he didn't think the body could produce.

Although I felt uncomfortable, I broached the subject of his final wishes. He did not want to die in the hospital; he wanted to die at home. He wanted to be cremated, and his ashes were to be buried with our late uncle, the pilot.

He said it so casually—I didn't know how to respond. I'd rehearsed what to say when the time came to discuss his death, but I had expected it to be emotional. The casual tone confused me, and I stared at him, unable to say anything. My words of encouragement, the scriptures I'd selected, and the prayer I had prepared would have been out of place.

Eduardo was concerned about the date on which the inevitable would occur. He wanted to die on a date that would least impact our lives. It was the second day of December, and he agonized that it was happening at a time when the family typically celebrated many occasions. My birthday was a few days away, and he didn't want to die on that day or on any other family member's birthday. He didn't want to die on anyone's anniversary either.

He said he didn't want to linger and die during the holiday season because that would ruin Christmas for the family. I didn't think he would live to see Christmas, but of course I didn't tell him that.

I eventually pointed out that there could never be a good day for him to leave us. No matter when it happened, we would grieve, and no day or date could lessen our pain.

He asked the doctors to discharge him, but they advised against it because they didn't think he could manage his pain at home. A priest came by to pray for him and give him communion. When the priest left, Eduardo told me that he had a favor to ask of me. He asked me to tell our mother that his time had come and he needed her permission to go.

I was astonished by the request. Then it dawned on me that Eduardo had always been close to our mother, so it was understandable that he would want to sever the bond in a personal way.

Given our mother's condition, I didn't think she would understand. Eduardo was confident that she would, even if outwardly she did not appear to do so. Not only did he want me to tell her he was dying, he wanted me to deliver the message in person.

Reluctantly, I flew to Pereira the next day. It was a nice Saturday afternoon, and a neighbor was sitting outside with my mother. When I told the neighbor why I was there, she left in tears. I then had the difficult task of breaking the news to my mom. A part of me wished that nothing I said would register.

I took her hand, and in a quivering voice I delivered her son's message. She understood every word I said. She cried for a while, composed herself, and asked me to record a message for Eduardo.

Between sobs, she said Eduardo had been suffering far too long, so he had her permission to go. She prayed for him and asked God to have mercy on his soul and give him an easy passage. In conclusion, she said there was nothing left on earth for Eduardo or for her, and she assured him that they would soon meet again in a much better place.

I don't think there can be anything more heart-wrenching than listening to a mother tell her son that it is okay to let go of life. When she stopped talking, I rushed over and held her. Time stood still as we cried together.

After delivering that kind of news, I did not want to leave my mother by herself. However, I had to get back to Eduardo. Every hour counted.

I returned to Bogota to find Eduardo at home. He wasn't expecting me to get back till the following day, so he was surprised when I showed up. A few of his friends were visiting, and he seemed to be enjoying their company.

When the visitors left, I told Eduardo about the trip and played our mother's message. He sobbed and reached out as if to touch her. When the recording ended, he curled up and rocked back and forth. His body convulsed, and he cried a deep throaty cry as he pleaded with God for more time. "I'm not ready to die," he said over and over again.

He asked me why he had to leave us so soon. Once again I was ill-prepared. I didn't have the answers to his questions. What philosophy could I have shared? I was not standing on the brink of death wondering what lay ahead. I was not dealing with the notion of leaving my loved ones behind. How could I possibly have understood what he was going through?

I cradled him, and we cried together. When he had no energy left, he lay back against the couch and stared at the ceiling. After what seemed like hours, I helped him to his new room. His wife had moved him yet again. She'd taken his mattress out of the den and placed it in a smaller room.

No matter how much we tried, Eduardo couldn't get down low enough to lie on the mattress. I tried to carry him, and we crashed into a wall. He was over six feet tall, and picking him up was a challenge for my small frame. He started crying again and apologized for being a burden.

I dragged in the mattress from my bed and placed it on top of Eduardo's. I stacked a few pillows on the mattresses, and even then it was difficult for him to lower himself onto the bed. I had to give him a piggyback, squat, and then roll him onto the bed.

With all the commotion, I thought his wife would come and help us. She didn't; she either slept right through the noise or chose to ignore us. Eduardo had definitely been better off in the hospital where he had had a medical team to care for him.

I was heartbroken to think how much he must have suffered emotionally in that home. I consoled him till he fell asleep, and then I covered him with a couple of blankets and stood over him. The big strapping man with a commanding presence was reduced to a helpless, quivering invalid.

I was angry, and only my love for Miriam kept me from marching into Eduardo's bedroom and beating up his so-called wife. My brother did not deserve to be treated so poorly in his own home. The woman had taken everything from him in the divorce and strategically worked her way back into his life when he was vulnerable. She'd remarried him and moved into his condominium. She was sleeping in his bed while he was on the floor.

I went to my room, fell on my knees and prayed for my brother. I was unsure what to ask for. Seeing what he had to deal with, it seemed unfair to ask God to extend his life. On the other hand, I couldn't ask God to take him away from us.

I prayed for wisdom to keep my mouth shut so I would not jeopardize my relationship with my niece. I was frustrated that night, and I pounded my pillow for hours.

Chapter Thirty-Five

First thing in the morning, I made Eduardo breakfast. He barely touched the food. He was weak, and although his legs looked bigger, the rest of him seemed to have shrunk even more overnight. I helped him to the couch, made him comfortable, and then called Alberto via Skype. I stepped out of the room so they could talk privately. I did not hear what they said, but I could hear both of them crying.

Even though Eduardo's death seemed imminent, I went to town to rent a hospital bed. I was determined not to let him go through the humiliation of trying to get down onto a stack of mattresses again. Even if it was for only one night, I wanted him to sleep in a bed.

The medical supply store did not have a bed readily available. The manager made a few calls and promised to deliver one in twenty-four hours. "I don't have twenty-four hours!" I recall yelling at the man as I stormed out in tears. I was racing against time.

There was only one other shop that rented hospital beds, and they didn't have one either. I will never forget my desolation as I sat outside that store and cried. I felt we had all failed Eduardo. I blamed myself for not visiting him sooner. I could have rented a bed and made provision for his meals. I knew I would never forgive myself if I watched my brother die on a makeshift bed.

I returned to Eduardo's home just in time to see paramedics put him in the elevator. They were carrying him in a plastic chair because their stretcher was too wide for the elevator. He lived on the sixteenth floor, and carrying him down the stairs on a gurney was out of the question.

He was trembling and sweating profusely. His legs seemed more swollen than they had been an hour earlier. He looked up and told me that his wife had called the ambulance. Though it was his wish to die at home, he did not complain about being sent back to the hospital. I did not question the decision either; I was relieved that he would have a bed.

I caught a cab and followed the ambulance to the hospital. By the time I got there, Eduardo was in excruciating pain and his breathing was labored. He doubled over and groaned each time the pain wracked his body. I begged the nurses to tend to him quickly. He was given oxygen and pain medication, and that helped somewhat.

He lay back quietly but expectantly. The time was near, and, like me, he was probably wondering what would happen next. He was about to leave the world he knew and find out what was on the other side.

He drifted in and out of consciousness, and every time I thought he was leaving me, he would open his eyes, shake his head, and take deep breaths. He was refusing to die. I held his hand and said, "Don't hold on. You are tired, and it is okay to go."

With all his strength, he grabbed both my hands, propped himself up, and said angrily, "Don't say goodbye to me." How do you respond to that? I just stood and stared helplessly at my brother. The appointed day had come. He didn't want to go, but there was nothing anyone could do to stop the inevitable. It was a journey he had to take and one he had to face alone.

For hours, I sat quietly with Eduardo. It was surreal. I was keeping vigil with my brother while we waited for his death. His life was drawing to a close, and I was watching the last few pages of the final chapter turn. Between groans, he told me how much he wanted to live. He wondered out loud what death would be like and whether he would be able to see us from the other side.

Talking to someone about their death is difficult, even when it is imminent. I was squirming in my seat, desperate to find the right things to say. His voice grew weaker and was eventually reduced to a whisper. I held him and prayed over him. He couldn't speak, so he nodded in agreement. I tried to sing hymns, but I choked on the words.

His wife showed up, followed by his son and daughter. Since he could have only two visitors at a time, I left the room so they could talk to him. We took turns sitting with him, and I prayed that I would be by his side when he passed away.

By late afternoon he was agitated, so the doctor decided to increase his dose of morphine. We knew that once he was sedated, he could easily slip away. I gripped his hands a little tighter. He managed to ask for a priest and gestured to the doctor to hold off the medication.

Even though the anointing of the sick had been administered to him the previous week, Eduardo wanted the sacrament again. I was with him when the priest arrived and gave him the last rites. He was attentive, and the prayers made him peaceful. He'd always had strong faith, and I drew consolation from that. I believed that once his last painful hours on earth were over, he would be in heaven with God.

When the priest left, Eduardo and I hugged and he gave me a kiss. He started to say something, but the doctor showed up and interrupted him. He patted my hand and gave me a big smile. I told him to hold the thought till I returned. He nodded, and I hurried to get out of the doctor's way.

"Thank you!" Eduardo called out as I was leaving the room. I spun around in surprise. It was the strongest his voice had been in hours.

All four of us were allowed back in the room when the doctor was done. Eduardo's eyes were open, but he did not move. He'd spoken to me less than five minutes prior, and I thought he would say something more, but he didn't say a word.

We took turns praying and saying our goodbyes. Eduardo did not acknowledge us; his eyes were fixed on one corner of the room. I thanked him for being a good son and brother. I praised him for putting up a good fight. I wished him well and asked him to tell our dad that I still missed him.

I knew Eduardo had to be thinking about our mother, so I promised him that I would take good care of her. When I said that, he turned his head, glanced at me and shut his eyes. He never opened them again.

He nodded once in response to a nurse's questions, but other than that, there was no more communication from him. He lost consciousness around five o'clock that afternoon.

We continued to talk to him, hoping he would know that we were there. I knelt at his bedside and prayed that angels would show him the way home.

Shortly before nine o'clock that night, I stepped into the waiting room so his son and daughter could be with him. Minutes later, I heard my niece scream, and I knew Eduardo was gone.

I rushed into the room to find his wife trying unsuccessfully to console her children. I climbed onto the bed and held my brother's lifeless body. We wailed so much, a nurse shut the door to contain the noise.

I refused to leave the room when the others were ushered out. I wouldn't let the nurses get Eduardo ready for the morgue; I couldn't bear to think of him lying on a cold slab. "He'll be cold in the morgue." I pleaded with them.

I screamed when the nurses first referred to Eduardo as "the body," and I clung to him till they pried my hands off. I guess grief can make a person irrational.

A nurse held me while another removed the tubes and cleaned the body. Once they were done, they let us look at him. I threw myself on my brother's chest and stayed there till I was dragged out of the room.

When they wheeled the body away, I tried to block the path of the gurney. Someone restrained me, but I broke free and chased the attendant until he went through a door that promptly shut behind him.

My niece and nephew led me to a couch, and we all tried to come to terms with what had just occurred. I still don't recall how I got from the ward to the car.

After battling cancer for seven long years, Eduardo gave up the fight. He died on the fourth of December, one day before my birthday. I had the difficult task of notifying the family, and with every call I relived the agony.

It was painful to break the news to my mother. She'd lost two sons in as many years, and I worried that Eduardo's death would push her over the edge. She alternated between weeping and talking to Eduardo as though she could see him.

I helped Miriam and her mother plan the funeral, and that is one of the most difficult things a person can do. Words cannot describe the feeling when an undertaker carries on about your loved one's "remains."

We coordinated the service with Eduardo's church. I selected hymns our father used to sing and some that our mother sang following his death. The Spanish versions of "God be with you till we meet again," "The strife is over, the battle done," and "Now the laborer's task is over" were on my list. The lyrics of such songs are powerful, but they become even more poignant when you lose someone you love dearly. The words made my heart heavier and affirmed the separation. My brother was gone, and all we had was the hope that we would one day reunite with him on the other side.

There was a consensus not to take our mother to the funeral, and with the exception of Marcela, all my siblings were present. Marcela experienced what I had dreaded for many years. She didn't see Eduardo when he was sick, and she couldn't attend his funeral because she still didn't have a green card.

Rafael came alone and sat by himself the entire time. I don't believe he got close enough to see his brother's body. The two never did reconcile.

Those who didn't see Eduardo in his latter stages were shocked to see how much he'd wasted away. We didn't just mourn his loss, we grieved over the suffering he endured for so long.

I was able to sit through the service, but I practically threw myself to the ground when the body was taken away to be cremated. Rosalinda was hysterical, and even my brothers sobbed loudly.

The family received guests at the church hall, but Rafael did not join us. He left immediately after the service without speaking to anyone.

As Eduardo requested, we buried his ashes with our uncle. I will never forget December 2011. Christmas was not the same. It was the first one without Eduardo and the second consecutive holiday season where we were in mourning. Almost every conversation was about Eduardo and Alejandro.

Chapter Thirty-Six

$\mathcal{W}$e somehow got through the next few months. In September of 2012, almost two years after his disappearance, Alejandro's daughters held a memorial service in Montreal. They had resigned themselves to the fact that he was dead and they would never find his body.

Alberto and I were there. It was a touching ceremony, followed by a reception during which former colleagues and friends shared memories of Alejandro. They told hilarious stories about his antics. They also shared accounts of extremely kind acts he had randomly performed. I laughed and cried at the same time.

One question came up over and over again: how could anyone kill Alejandro? He was so personable and had a disarming way about him. His friends were surprised that he hadn't been able to negotiate with his captors. They thought that if anybody could have talked their way out of a bad situation, it would have been Alejandro. They asked the same questions that I had asked of his ex-wife, and they didn't like the answers she'd given me any more than I did.

Those who knew Evelyn agreed that taking her to Colombia was a step in the wrong direction and probably Alejandro's undoing. It was difficult to look at his daughters, listen to tributes, and watch videos of his life without breaking down a few times.

It is painful to have a loved one senselessly ripped from you. Not having a body to bury makes it twice as difficult to find closure. All we had to go by were our suppositions and Alejandro's continued absence. We had to make an educated guess on the month in which he might have died. We didn't have a death certificate, a grave to visit, or a headstone on which to inscribe our final thoughts.

The day before we left Montreal, we got a surprise. A former neighbor brought us a sea trunk that Alejandro had left in his care. It was filled with sculptures, abstract paintings, and sketches.

The artwork captured the very essence of Alejandro. Years earlier, he'd lived in a remote area of Vancouver Island with a cat and a young bear. Many of his paintings were of the island and the two animals. It was easy to see how much he loved his "pets" and how difficult it had been for him to leave them behind. We were teary-eyed by the time we finished going through the trunk.

Later that year, Alejandro's younger daughter and I went to Taganga. The police escorted us up the mountains to the area where he had been building. Though we didn't go to the construction site, we were close enough to see the cabins. They were partially covered by overgrown grass and appeared to be empty.

The place was so quiet we resorted to whispering. My niece and I stood on the mountainside and stared at what could have been. When the police were ready to leave, I took one final look at Alejandro's dream. He was right; the location would have been perfect for retreats.

The police dropped us off in Taganga, and we went to the beach. It was easy to see why the area lured my brother and ultimately cost him his life. Even though we were just yards from his house, we did not go near it. The infectious laugh that had reverberated through the house was gone forever.

Without warning, I became agitated. A part of me wanted to go to the cluster of homes near Alejandro's house, knock on doors, ask questions, and pass on a message to the community. In a small Colombian town, my message would have reached everyone.

I wanted to tell them that they all had my brother's blood on their hands. I wanted to point out that those who knew what had happened and remained silent were just as guilty as those who had had a part in his disappearance.

I was angry, and if I'd known where to buy a bull horn in Taganga, I would have bought one that day. I would have charged up the hill and rained curses on the people and on their homes.

My niece was the voice of reason that afternoon. She stopped me from doing anything drastic and made me focus on the good times I had shared with my brother in Taganga. I thought about the long walks we took with Leon and the dogs and recalled the many hours we spent on the beach talking about Alejandro's plans for the future.

Contrary to what she expected, nothing spiritual drew my niece to her father's grave. We left Taganga before dark, and I knew I would never return.

Chapter Thirty-Seven

$\mathcal{I}$ flew back to Maryland and found myself in the middle of a crisis. Rosalinda's bags were packed, and she was ready to go back to Alabama. I needed someone to put Leon on the school bus in the mornings and meet him when he was dropped off in the afternoon. I begged Rosalinda to give me time to make other arrangements, but she refused. She took off the next day, leaving me frantic.

I made several calls, but I couldn't find anyone to help me. I went downstairs to walk off my frustration, and that was when it dawned on me to ask the doorman for help. It wasn't the best solution, but it would keep me from losing my job.

We already had a good relationship with Mr. Jennings, and Leon was comfortable around him. I had found out much earlier that the elderly man was homeless, and since then I helped him whenever I could. Marcela and I often gave him hot meals, and at least once a month I gave him food and toiletries that I collected from friends.

Mr. Jennings worked full-time in our building; he was there six days a week and usually worked double shifts. Unfortunately, he had severe health issues and was forced to spend his income on medical bills.

He was happy to help and got emotional when I said I would pay him. I left Leon with him the very next day, and we were down in the lobby before 6 a.m. every morning. Leon would immediately climb onto a couch and cover his head with a blanket. I felt really bad about waking him up so early, especially since the bus did not pick him up until 9 a.m.

For the first couple of days, I cried after dropping Leon off with Mr. Jennings. After that, I looked on the bright side. Some parents had to wake their kids up at dawn and drag them to the bus stop.

Mr. Jennings put Leon on the school bus, met him when he was dropped off, and kept him occupied until I got home from work. My child spent so much time in the lobby that every resident got to know him by name. Though I couldn't afford to pay Mr. Jennings much money, he was very appreciative of what I gave him each week.

The arrangement was supposed to be only a short-term solution, yet it went on for months. Leon's teacher called me over and over again because he was always sleepy in class.

At first I made up excuses, but then she started asking not-so-subtle questions about my personal life. When I was hauled in to meet with the teacher, a counselor, and the school psychologist, I knew I had to find a better option. The last thing

I wanted was for the school to call Child Protective Services and start an investigation. Officious social workers have been known to disrupt lives for lesser reasons.

I had to find an affordable babysitter and figure out how to drop Leon off in the mornings and still get to work on time. While I frantically tried to find a resolution, Marcela resolved the issue. It was serendipitous.

Over the years, she'd repeatedly brought up the issue of sponsorship so she could become a legal resident of the United States. Her employers started the process but always had one excuse or another for not completing it.

Not being able to attend Eduardo's funeral really upset Marcela and made her more aggressive in her demands. Her employers did not appreciate that and became verbally abusive. They piled on more duties, even though she was already working long hours, seven days a week.

When I called to resolve the issue, they got defensive. They told me that they had no intentions of sponsoring Marcela. My sister was devastated. She'd held onto the job for over ten years, just so she could get a green card. Once they took that off the table, there was no point in staying.

Marcela packed her bags and walked off the job with her head held high. I had mixed emotions when I picked her up. I was proud of her for standing up to her employers, yet I was apprehensive. She hadn't given them notice, and I was worried that they would be vindictive and report her to the immigration authorities. I was also concerned about how long it would take her to find another job.

Having Marcela back at home was a timely blessing. I did not have to wake Leon up at dawn, and he didn't have to spend hours in the lobby each day. Above all, I had no more complaints from his school.

Shortly after Marcela came home, Melissa and her dog moved in with us. With four of us and a pet in the condo, it could have been chaotic. Being obsessive about cleanliness, Marcela kept the home spotless.

I put notices in our lobby and found her odd jobs. She took care of a few kids in the area and cleaned homes in Bethesda. She made more money than she did when she worked seven days a week. She was also happier than she'd been in years.

Just when we were settling into our new routine, my brother Rodrigo called from Canada. He was beside himself. His wife had just been diagnosed with breast cancer. She had battled the disease earlier, and after four years in remission, it was back.

Leon and I went to visit Rodrigo and his family. Once again, Marcela was unable to leave the country. One of her friends had an elaborate plan to take her across the border and into Canada, but I talked her out of taking the risk.

My sister-in-law was in a lot of pain, and it reminded me of Eduardo's struggle. The difference was that while Eduardo had to fend for himself in his end-stage, Rodrigo barely left his wife's side. He'd taken a leave of absence so he could give her his undivided attention.

The cancer was aggressive, and within weeks my sister-in-law succumbed to the disease. Rodrigo fell apart. Alberto and I flew to Calgary to be with him and his daughters.

I have never seen a man cry as much as Rodrigo did. He seemed dazed throughout the funeral, and he wanted to go back to work immediately afterward. When he called his employer, he was told he no longer had a job. After fifteen years with the company and at the most difficult time of his life, they let him go.

I was very concerned about Rodrigo's state of mind, but thankfully, his daughters stepped in and gave him the support he needed.

Chapter Thirty-Eight

I still feel a twinge in my heart when I consider that I was only hours away from starting medical school all those years ago. I can't help wondering how different my life could have been. When I hear doctors paged over the intercom in hospitals, it stirs emotions buried deep within me. A lifetime ago, I fantasized about being paged to take care of my patients.

While I cannot help those sentiments, I have come to terms with the fact that studying medicine was not in the cards for me. I may not be able to improve the health of hundreds of people, but I have been able to touch two lives in a very special way.

The little boy whom doctors gave a slim chance of survival is now a young man. Emanuel has been healthy since his early battle with leukemia. He routinely sees his doctors, and so far all is well. He is getting ready to go to college and has his sights set on Stanford University in California. He wants to be an attorney some day. I thought he would opt for medicine so he could help others, but he is not interested in that field. I guess he has been in and out of doctor's offices for most of his life, so he has no desire to work in one.

Begging for money to save Emmanuel's life was worth it, and I would do it all over again if I had to. I recently signed over to him, the medical account I had opened to collect donations for his treatment. The account had $50,000 in it, and Emmanuel will use it toward college. Carmilo, who gave bone marrow to save his little brother's life, will soon graduate from college.

How could an immigrant with a limited knowledge of the English language have mobilized so many people to help a child far way in Colombia? I know God's hand was at work every step of the way.

I will always be grateful to Josh for motivating me to do something about Emanuel's illness. He could have allowed me to wallow in helplessness. Instead, he taught me to be resourceful, and that lesson will remain with me forever.

My beloved Melissa, who was not supposed to have cognitive skills, speaks two languages and is studying culinary arts in a trade school. Her quality of life is beyond what the doctors predicted. She recently moved back to her father's house, but she still spends plenty of time with me.

Melissa has been a blessing in my life, and she will always be my inspiration. Her older brother Adam is a very successful businessman, and I know Laura would have been proud of him. Karen still struggles with their mother's death and refuses to talk about it. She is more reclusive than most people her age, but then again, her contemporaries haven't endured what she has.

Josh is an amazing father, and he does all he can to fill the void Laura left. He and I often talk about her, and on each anniversary of her death, we visit her grave. Thinking about Laura sometimes brings a smile to my face, and some days I cry for her. I will always be thankful for having had that lady in my life. Now that the kids are older, I hope Josh remarries. He deserves happiness.

Grandma and Grandpa Levenson have passed on, and we miss them. Their deaths were difficult for Melissa to accept; she doesn't understand why her loved ones are taken away. She rarely hears from her maternal grandparents, but that does not surprise me. They weren't close to their daughter. Adam tried unsuccessfully to maintain a relationship with them, and he now reaches out only on birthdays and on holidays.

Marcela still lives with me, and I am thankful for her company. She has found a church with a large Latino population, and she is very active in the parish. She looks forward to Sundays, when she can attend mass and socialize.

She no longer feels isolated because she is surrounded by others who are just like her. She and her friends belong to a Latino world that will never be a part of mainstream America. In essence, they have created a country within the country, and for political and economic reasons, significant changes have been made to accommodate that population. If I had any doubt before, I now know for a fact that she will never learn to speak English.

It has been fifteen years since Marcela first arrived in the United States. She still doesn't have a green card, and she worries that she could eventually be deported. Worse still, she fears that she may never see our mother again.

Rosalinda lives in Alabama with her daughter. She is still draped in discouragement and pines for the job she lost and the pension she didn't receive. My sister found herself in a dark corner and made it her home. She needs professional counseling, but she is offended when we bring up the subject. Latinos generally tend to think there is a stigma attached to depression and mental illness. Seeing a mental health professional is tantamount to declaring yourself crazy, or *loco*, as we say.

Rosalinda's situation has taught me that challenges are usually temporary unless we choose to make them permanent. Taking no action to change your circumstance ensures that you remain in it. I try to improve my lot, even if it is only by the smallest of margins.

My son Leon is an outspoken child with a love of life and the outdoors. His dream is to create video games and sell them all over the world. With the money he makes, he plans to buy a Ferrari and a mansion. He can't make up his mind whether to buy me my own house or allow me to live in his mansion with him!

Just as my father listened to my dreams, I love to hear about my son's aspirations. Thank God for the opportunities this country offers! As long as he works hard, he can achieve his goals.

In my own small way, I've carved out a good life for my son. Some may even say that Leon lives a life of privilege. He is surrounded by love, we live in a nice area, and I am able to meet all his needs. Our public school system is the best in the country, and he is getting as good an education as kids get in private schools.

Thanks to my job, Leon has travelled all over the United States. He has been to Disney World, Hawaii, Niagara Falls, Yellowstone National Park, Martha's Vineyard, Aspen, and many other popular places. We've been to Canada, Spain, Finland, France, England, and Italy, with more trips to come.

Naturally, as Leon grew older he asked questions about his father. Years earlier when I made the decision to have a child through unconventional means, I did not think it would be as difficult to have "the talk." I eventually gathered courage and told him the truth. He listened, asked a couple of questions, and then got up and left the room.

Marcela had been out of the house when Leon and I had had the conversation, but the minute she returned, she sensed the incredible tension and guessed what had transpired. She quickly left again, and to date she has not asked me or Leon any questions pertaining to that episode.

Leon was sullen for the next couple of days and politely refused everything I offered him. He wouldn't even eat when I was home. I was heartbroken and didn't know what to do. Three days after we talked, he told me that even though I had dashed his hopes of living with both of his parents someday, he was okay with the information. I was relieved!

I am eternally grateful to Eduardo and Alberto for giving me the courage to have a child. Having Leon was the best thing that ever happened to me. It hasn't been easy being a single parent, and I wouldn't recommend it for everyone, but it was the right decision for me.

We miss Eduardo, and I now understand why he was concerned about dying on the "wrong day." He died a day before my birthday, and I have relived his passing every year. The entire first week of December will probably always bring me sad memories.

Every time Miriam and I are together, we reminisce about her father. She now has two children, and thankfully, the second pregnancy was a much easier one.

We never did find Alejandro's body, and I may never know the whole truth surrounding his disappearance. I don't believe Alberto has told me everything he knows, Rafael is still estranged from the family, and Eduardo took his information to the grave.

After months of pushing the Colombian police to find Alejandro's abductors, the Canadian Embassy in Bogota gave up. The house in Taganga is still vacant, and the incomplete project stands in the mountains of Parque Tayrona. The cartel will probably wait until it is safe to sell the properties to unsuspecting buyers. Some poor souls will walk into the same trap my brother fell into.

Evelyn never gave us the missing pieces of information; her story became more and more convoluted. Alberto and

Rodrigo tried to be patient with her in hopes of learning more. They too finally gave up.

Alberto still lives in Finland and has a very successful career. Leon and I recently spent a week with him at his vacation home on the Turkish Riviera. He has a pensive air about him, and it is easy to see that he still grieves for his brothers.

Rodrigo continues to struggle with the loss of his wife. He fears that, because of his age, he may not find another job in Canada. He is contemplating a return to Colombia but is skeptical that he can adapt to the way of life. We've been gone for so long, we are hesitant to go back to the land of our birth.

My nemesis Diego still lives at home and probably will for the rest of his life. He is still a problem, but I have been told that every family has a Diego. It is hard to believe that he and I were born to the same parents and raised in the same home. Juan Carlos moved out and lives with his wife and children.

My mother is still "hanging in there," as they say. The Alzheimer's disease has progressed, and she confuses things from different eras. She repeats herself and rambles about riding horses in her youth. She never talked about horses when she was of sound mind, so I wonder if there are still unshared secrets locked away in her head. Every now and then she picks up a phone to call Eduardo and Alejandro. Thankfully, she no longer asks for the two daughters she abandoned.

My estranged sisters never reopened a dialogue, and we have come to terms with that. It was probably the best way for them to deal with their shock and, perhaps, embarrassment.

I don't know how I would have felt in their shoes, so I don't judge them. I have closed that chapter, and I wish them peace in their lives.

My friends Yolanda and Gladys still live in Virginia, and both of them are now legal residents. Yolanda is married; she is a stay-at-home mom raising three adoptive children. Gladys wanted to go back to practicing pharmacy, but by the time she received her green card, too much time had elapsed. To get back in the profession, she would have to go back to school for a few years. She now runs a successful small business. I have the utmost respect for those two ladies, two Latinas who refused to be pigeon-holed.

Esme returned to Colombia and is working in a school founded by her sister. She is still married to Antonio. In spite of all his schemes, Antonio couldn't make ends meet in the United States, so he finally packed his bags and went to join his wife.

I ran into Giovanna about three years ago, and I was shocked to hear that she was still with the Argentine family and still didn't have a green card. The kids were in college, Dr. Morales had passed away, and Señora Morales was preparing to sell the home. She could no longer afford a housekeeper, so Giovanna was looking for another job.

Señora Morales was about to let her faithful worker go without ever having petitioned for her green card. I wondered if the woman had any remorse for stringing Giovanna along for so many years.

Chapter Thirty-Nine

I consider it a blessing to be a citizen of two great nations. I have lived a greater part of my life in the United States and call this country home. If I had to do it all over again, would I do things differently?

The answer is a resounding yes. I would exhaust all options in my native home before moving to the United States or to any other country. I would leave Colombia only if I were going straight to school and had the proper immigration documents in hand. I would have specific goals and a timeline in which to achieve them. After that, I would go back home.

I wish I could share this nugget of wisdom with young people everywhere: Especially where education is free, take advantage of it and go as far as you can. You may not have fancy classrooms or the latest technologies, but remember that even with the sparsest of resources, others have achieved greatness. Go to college or learn a trade. After that, explore the opportunities at home before heading for what you deem greener pastures. If you do leave, have a plan and know when to backtrack.

In retrospect, I should have stayed in Colombia and finished college. When my plans to attend medical school fell through, I should have returned to the university in Pereira. I didn't necessarily have to continue the engineering program; I could have changed direction.

Friends and schoolmates who stayed in Colombia are much better off than those of us who left. Those who graduated from college now hold prominent positions. Those who didn't go to college married college graduates and live comfortably. They have nannies, housekeepers, gardeners, and chauffeurs. They have no desire to leave the country, unless it is for business or for family vacations. Their progress may have come slowly, but their perseverance paid off.

It is a common stereotype that in order to have any semblance of a good life, Latin Americans must cross the border into the United States. Unfortunately, Latinos too believe that erroneous notion. For the uneducated Latino, it may be the best alternative. For those with opportunities in their countries, coming to America may offer a short-term fix, but it is not necessarily the optimum solution. Sadly, most immigrants only come to that realization after years of floundering in the system.

Especially for professionals, moving to a different country without the right papers can stunt progress. It usually means setting aside skills, qualifications, dignity, and even status. Those who must first seek work permits, learn a new language, and obtain licenses in order to work in their field are twice as likely to be disillusioned. If things don't go as planned, instead of achieving more, they lose everything. Time passes, licenses expire, and education is rendered useless.

Prejudice is an issue that I deal with in my new country. Skin color features prominently in what you are allowed to have, and it often supersedes a person's capabilities. Even though I have been working as a volunteer in Leon's school for the last five years, I am "not qualified" for a paid position doing the exact same job. People that I trained have been hired while I patiently await my turn. It's just another price you pay for leaving home.

As an immigrant, I have had to endure other people's ignorance. Ironically, it is usually those at the bottom of the social ladder who are most condescending. They are narrow minded, lack education, and do not know enough about the world to appreciate diversity.

Animosity towards Latinos is on the rise, and political rhetoric has played a major part in that. People tend to think all Latinos are illegal immigrants looking for handouts from the government. It is true that many are undocumented, but most of us are hard-working, and we constitute a large percentage of the workforce. I am convinced that if every Latino in the country were to go on strike for two consecutive days, the system would be severely impacted.

It saddens me that I cannot incubate my son from the cruel realities in this country. I can't pretend that bigotry does not exist. We encounter it daily, and sometimes it is so glaring, even young children see it.

Latinos endure racism from all the other ethnicities. Generally speaking, Whites look down on us, Blacks despise us, and Asians distrust us. Those realities will not change any time soon. My job is to educate Leon on the harsh facts and give him the tools to rise above them.

To make matters worse, Latinos discriminate against each other. Puerto Ricans never let us forget that US citizenship is their birthright. Argentines are supposedly European; to hear them tell it, they are Spaniards and Italians. Cubans claim overall superiority. The rest of us also draw lines in the sand. We distinguish between Mexicanos, Bolivianos, Peruanos, Salvadoreños, and so on. We temporarily drop those distinctions when we need to unite against a common adversary. Then, we are one race. *Somos todos primos*: we are all cousins.

The debate continues about Latin American children crossing the border in record numbers, and I am frequently asked my opinion on the subject. I think it is a travesty. How many of them will be adopted into loving families, get an education, and live the American dream? Opportunists will take kids in not out of compassion but because of the money foster parents are paid.

American-born children fall through the cracks in the foster-care system every day. Will social workers advocate for Hispanic children who are here illegally? These children will be marginalized; they will be conveniently ignored and eventually forgotten.

Many of these kids will probably be placed with Spanish-speaking families. While that may seem logical or ideal, it could isolate them and prevent them from flourishing in their communities. Given my experience with Antonio and the Morales family, I suspect that some kids will be exploited. They will be treated like servants and used as cheap labor.

Worse still, they could be sexually exploited. Women are raped in Latino communities every day. While many of those crimes go unreported, rape crisis centers probably still see a significant number of women from that population.

These children could end up in the homes of predators. They don't know the language, and they don't understand the system. They can be manipulated with the threat of deportation to keep them in line.

With the raging sex trade and global human trafficking, who is tracking these children? Pedophiles are known to travel to countries where they can exploit young children with no ramifications. They don't have far to look now. We have droves of young children in the country with inadequate systems in place to take care of them. Hundreds more trek across Latin America every day. These children are easy prey, and it frightens me when I think of all the things that could happen to them along the way.

I will never understand how parents can send their unaccompanied children to another country and to nobody in particular. By and large, these children are not fleeing war-torn areas. They are ostensibly coming to the United States to get away from drug violence.

Violence reigns supreme in the streets of Chicago, Los Angeles, Washington DC, and many other US cities. Inner-city parents will attest to that. They see drug-related violence every day, yet they do not ship their children to other states or across the border to Canada. It would be preposterous and utterly irresponsible.

Children are much more vulnerable when they travel thousands of miles and across borders by themselves. There would have to be famine or a natural disaster for me to let go of my child. Even then, it would only be a temporary separation. Not war, poverty, or the pursuit of fortune will make me send my underage child into the unknown. We would flee together or not at all. No matter how bad economic conditions may be, my child will remain with me. He will eat what I eat and sleep where I sleep. As a mother, I need to nurture my son, comfort him, and let him know he is loved.

The poorest of Latino parents shower their children with affection and terms of endearment. They are *mija* or *mijo, bonita, querida, mi amor, pappito, mamita* and so on. We constantly hug and kiss our children; we sing folk songs of our love for them. How do you just rip that bond? How will these children fare with strangers who may not even speak their language? I can only imagine how lonely and abandoned some of them must feel.

How and when will these children be reunited with their families? Many of them may never see their parents again. The very young ones will soon forget what their family members look like.

How do you help a four-year-old find his mother and father who live on another continent? How do you find the right Maria Lopez or Hector Gonzales in Santiago or San José? Many villages, towns and cities across Latin America have the same names. Where do you begin?

I am certain that some families are in dire straits and send their children away as a last resort. It is not a popular thing to say among Latinos, but the majority of parents involved see this as a way to guarantee their own future entry into the United States.

There is nothing wrong with leaving home in search of opportunities; I did it too. However, we reverse the laws of nature when the very young have to make sacrifices so they can pave paths for their parents.

In my opinion, all the governments involved have failed these children. How do municipalities watch a multitude of children trudge across countries and do nothing about it? Letting them live in America is not synonymous with improving their lives. A parent's love, guidance, and protection are priceless and essential in a child's upbringing.

The United States could potentially become a breeding ground for a future generation of bitter and disaffected immigrants. These children are coming here with certain expectations. Top on the list is the hope that their parents can join them soon. They will one day clamor in the streets if that does not happen.

Arabelle:

Instead of supporting the mass exodus of children from Latin America, the respective countries should address and fix the problems at the source. International organizations and the "first world" countries should consider helping families in that region so parents don't feel compelled to send their children away.

Chapter Forty

isappointment, prejudice, depression, terminal illness, abduction, murder, suicide. Some of the sorrows I have encountered along the way. They are the building blocks that have shaped my life. Individually, any one of those experiences could have broken my spirit. Collectively and bonded by the element of time, they form an almost impenetrable shell. They make me resilient and give me the courage to forge ahead.

I am at a point where I no longer curse the storm. As the saying goes, I have learned to dance in the rain. I am not complacent about mediocrity, and I haven't stopped dreaming, but whatever my circumstances, I strive to be happy.

There are still many things I need to live comfortably. Rather than dwell on what I can't have or didn't get, I give thanks for what I have. I pray that we can one day move into a home that gives us a little more space. Until then, it is Marcela, Leon, Melissa, her dog, and me in the one-bedroom condominium. It gets crowded, but we have a roof over our heads, and I am happy to be surrounded by love.

I don't make much money, but I live within my means. I still keep track of every penny I spend. I have a little in savings, and I have a college fund for my son. I have good credit, and if I ever needed to, I could borrow from a bank. When my old minivan finally broke down, I walked confidently into my credit union and applied for a car loan. The timing was right, and I was able to purchase a fairly new truck for much less than its actual value. It was the best feeling ever! I know people who were born and raised in the United States but will never know that kind of stability.

Life at the airport is tolerable. We continue to get inner-city youth, and I have learned to work beside them. I no longer fret over the actions of the troublesome ones; they don't last on the job anyway. In my early days working at National Airport, I thought most inner city youth were overly aggressive, but I now feel differently. Some outstanding agents have come from the same population, and they have reshaped my views. I guess I got to know them, and in the process dropped my generalizations and misconceptions.

I am eligible to walk away from the airline with flight benefits for the rest of my life. I still desire to work in the medical field, and I would like to go to nursing school next year. I pray that I will finally have the opportunity to unlock some of the passion that has been jailed inside of me for years.

I would also like to promote tourism in Colombia someday. Over the years I have taken many friends back home, and they have invariably been amazed at the beauty of the country. I have come a long way from hurling information at co-workers; there are many people who genuinely want to hear about Colombia.

Looking back, the agents who made fun of my heritage did me a favor. They made me learn a lot more about my native home, and I know I could run an awesome program someday.

I believe that the tough experiences in my life are a part of God's master plan for me. He uses them to strengthen me and to prepare me for the next round of adversity. I no longer fear that word. Some of the best things in my life have come after adversity.

If Antonio hadn't kicked me out of their home, I might still be cleaning shopping malls for a living. If my Argentine employers hadn't treated me reprehensibly, I wouldn't have gone to work for the Levensons.

The Levensons were an answer to my prayers. However, I thank God that Laura cut the cord at the end of that season. It led to a job that allows me to see the world.

A failed car deal resulted in surplus money in my bank account. That enabled me to purchase my condominium. Housing prices soared shortly afterwards, and clearly the condo would have been out of my price range.

I was disappointed when my mother couldn't travel to Finland with me. Taking a co-worker instead led to the conversation about single parenthood and alternative methods of conception. That discussion ultimately led to my most precious gift.

I have at times felt like life's punching bag, and I used to think fate took delight in dangling good fortune just out of my reach. I've cried till I had no tears left, yet through it all I have found contentment.

Some people seemingly cruise on smooth roads all through their lives. Others, regardless of where they began, happen to take the right exits and merge onto smooth highways. Some of us, not for lack of trying, have a journey fraught with detours, bumpy roads, and dead ends. In spite of that, we too can enjoy the ride.

Our shoes may have holes in them, and our cars may sound like old locomotives, but that should not stop us from singing along the way. We cannot wait on perfection before we allow ourselves to be happy. It would be a shame to die without having lived fully.

I have now adopted a "panic only for a moment" approach to life. Though circumstances may initially hurt or scare me, I refuse to stay down. I get on my knees and ask for strength and the wisdom to effectively tackle difficulties. My philosophy is that if I can't solve a problem when I am calm, I certainly won't solve it when I am frazzled.

I could never have predicted the events in my past, but I do know that as long as I keep living there will be strife. I'll cross the bridges of hardship and sorrow when I get there. Until then, I am enjoying this journey called life.

Bigger and better may never come, and today might be the last of my tomorrows. I have *now*, the most precious and overlooked resource.

Epilogue

If your journey through life has been on smooth, well-lit roads, be patient with those still maneuvering around craters. Not everyone who lives on the dirt road chooses to be there; it is the hand that they were dealt. In their shoes, you might be no different.

Don't despise us when we plod along and slow you down. Be thankful for what you have and know that the difference is—the hand that you were dealt.

Acknowledgements

Arabella, thank you for letting me tell your story.

KDG and Sandra, thank you for your unwavering support.

Warren, thank you for being unrelenting.

Gerry and Lorraine, thank you.

CPSIA information can be obtained at www.ICGtesting.com
Printed in the USA
BVOW08s0310120916

461704BV00002B/6/P